A
DYER'S
Garden

FROM PLANT TO POT
GROWING DYES FOR NATURAL FIBERS

RITA BUCHANAN

INTERWEAVE PRESS

W9-CZT-551

A Dyer's Garden
Rita Buchanan

Design, Keith Rosenhagen/Graphic Relations
Yarn Photography, Joe Coca
All other photography, Rita Buchanan
Production, Marc McCoy Owens

Text copyright 1995, Rita Buchanan
Yarn photography copyright 1995, Joe Coca and Interweave Press
Other photography copyright 1995, Rita Buchanan

 Interweave Press, Inc.
201 East Fourth Street
Loveland, Colorado 80537 USA
www.interweave.com

All rights reserved.

Printed in Hong Kong by Sing Cheong

Buchanan, Rita.
    A dyer's garden/Rita Buchanan.
        p.   cm.
    Includes index.
    ISBN 1-883010-07-1 (pbk.)
    1. Dye plants.   2. Gardening.   3. Dyes and dyeing, Domestic.
I. Title
SB285.B79 1995
633.8'6—dc20   95-7382
                                                  CIP

12 11 10 9 8 7

■ *Contents* ■

INTRODUCTION
4

One
CHOOSING
WHICH PLANTS
TO GROW
9

Two
GETTING AND
GROWING
DYE PLANTS
13

Three
PLANNING A DYE
GARDEN
20

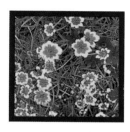

Four
THE BASICS
OF
DYEING WITH
PLANTS
32

Five
COLORS AND
COLORS
45

Six
A PORTFOLIO OF
DYE GARDEN
PLANTS
48

SUPPLIERS
110

BIBLIOGRAPHY
111

INDEX
112

■ *Introduction* ■

olor is one of the most attractive attributes of plants, but one of the most ephemeral. People come from around the country to see the blazing foliage of our New England forests in mid-October; those trees are bare by Halloween. All winter, I anticipate the yellowness of daffodils and forsythias in spring; they bloom and disappear in a few weeks. The cycle never stops—there's always something to look forward to, but it goes too fast for me. I want to slow it down, to embrace the colors and hold them somehow so I can savor them again and again. I have a way to do this. Using dyes from plants is my way of saving colors, of catching a rainbow and arranging it in a basket of yarn.

Dyeing with plants is an ancient craft, and the techniques are well established. It's possible to create a full spectrum of colors, and if properly chosen and applied, the dyes stand up to washing and light and fade slowly, if at all. We'll never know just how it happened that people discovered dye plants and figured out how to use them, but we know that dyers of old achieved spectacular results. Some of the incredible textiles that were dyed centuries ago have survived, and the colors of those antique tapestries, brocades, and embroideries are still impressively rich and varied. However, the invention of cheap, convenient synthetic dyes in the late 1800s eclipsed the use of natural dyes, and the craft of dyeing with plants nearly died out in the twentieth century. Then began a slow resurgence, and now in the 1990s, individual dyers around the world are working seriously with plants again, rediscovering old techniques and creating new ones. Dyeing with plants has a long history, but it has a dynamic present and a promising future, too.

What's the appeal of dyeing with plants? It attracts different people for different reasons. First is the beauty of the colors themselves. Then there's the simple pleasure of gathering leaves and flowers, and the alchemic magic of extracting a vivid blue dye from plain green indigo leaves or pulling distinctly different colors from a single dyepot by pretreating the yarn with different mordants. There's also the connection with history and the commitment to sustaining old traditions, the sense of mastery when a well-tested recipe produces the familiar and desired results, and the challenge of research when an undescribed plant or technique behaves unpredictably but shows tantalizing potential.

I relish all these aspects of dyeing, and even more, I enjoy the benefits of growing my own dye plants. Gardening isn't a traditional part of dyeing; most dyers are happy to gather local wild plants and/or purchase exotic dyestuffs (such as concentrated indigo, dried madder roots, or logwood chips) collected in other parts of the world. That approach is convenient but limited. By comparison, growing your own dye plants expands the whole process from start to finish and gives you more opportunity and greater reward. Tending a dye garden offers colors that you can't get from wild plants and a self-sufficient satisfaction that you can't get by using purchased dyestuffs. For me, the annual cycle of deciding what to grow, sowing seeds, watering and cultivating, watching the garden swell into a billow of flowers and foliage, then finally using the plants for dyeing is a crescendo of fulfillment and delight. Any captured color is a treasure, but the colors I save from my dye garden are most valuable of all.

COMMON QUESTIONS ABOUT DYES FROM PLANTS

Over the last ten years, I've given scores of slide shows and seminars about growing and using dye plants. Audience members ask some of the same questions every time. You might want to ask these questions, too, so I'll answer a few of them here.

Q: What colors can you get with dyes from plants? Are there any colors you can't get?
A: Many plants give shades of yellow, tan, brass, or gold. Those are the easiest colors to get. Shades of orange, brown, and a dull olive green are fairly available, too. Only a few plants give red dyes, and those reds usually have an orange or rusty tone. A few very special plants give blue dyes. Certain colors, including jet black, emerald green, turquoise, cotton-candy pink, royal purple, and garnet red, are rarely seen in dyes from plants. Some of these colors are readily obtained from other natural dye materials, such as cochineal insects (for reds and pinks) or orchil lichens (for pinks and purples), but not from plants.

Q: When you use dyes from plants, doesn't the yarn fade? And what happens if you wash the yarn?
A: Let's talk about washing first. I consider the last step in the dye process to be washing the yarn with warm water and dishwashing detergent, then rinsing it in plain water until no more color bleeds away. If yarn has been thoroughly washed and rinsed like this, it doesn't bleed in subsequent washings.

Fading due to light is a different issue. The colors from some plants do fade quickly, especially if the yarns are exposed to bright sunlight. Most dyers decide not to rely on those plants. Other plant dyes are quite permanent or fast, as dyers say, and fade very little or very slowly when exposed to light. Along with choosing reliable plants, careful measurement and application of mordants—the metallic compounds that are used in the dye process—is a critical aspect of producing fast colors. In my experience, the plants in this book all produce fast colors if they are prepared and applied according to directions. (Just to keep things in perspective, it's worth noting that synthetic dyes sometimes fade, too, when exposed to bright sun.)

Q: If you get a color you like, can you repeat the dye process to make the same color again?
A: You can usually get a similar color, if you use the same proportions of the same plant and the same yarn, and follow the same procedures, but there are so many variables to heed that it's very challenging to make an exact match. Nationwide, there's a handful of professional dyers who do produce a consistent line of yarns or goods dyed with natural dyes. These dyers have spent years developing their techniques. They generally use a limited number of very reliable plants (plus cochineal), often purchased in a dry, relatively concentrated form, and they pay close attention to all the details of the dye process.

Most amateur dyers—especially those of us who grow or gather our dye plants, rather than purchase them—don't care enough about reproducing specific colors to bother with all the measuring and record-keeping that's required. We usually take a more serendipitous approach. In fact, most of the dyers I know actually *prefer* to have each dye batch turn out different, because we like unique, one-of-a-kind results. Instead of consistency, we strive for diversity.

Q: Do you have recipes for dyeing?
A: I do follow and prescribe specific recipes for measuring and applying mordants, because using too little mordant may diminish the fastness of the color, and using too much sometimes harms the texture of the yarn.

Otherwise, the recipes I use for dyeing with plants are so simple that it's hard to even call them recipes—they're just guidelines, really, like the kind of guidelines you follow when you're baking potatoes, steaming broccoli, or scrambling eggs. I describe these guidelines on pages 39–41, and note any variations in the entries for individual dye plants. I suppose you could make more elaborate recipes for dyeing, but it isn't necessary, and it would make the dye process sound more complicated than it is.

Q: Are the colors you get from dyeing the same as you see in the plant?
A: Sometimes, but usually not. For example, goldenrod's yellow flowers give a range of yellow and gold dyes, but goldenrod's green leaves give shades of gold, tan, and brown—not green. In general, bright colored leaves or flowers are no guarantee of a plant's dye potential, and many excellent dye plants actually look quite drab.

Q: How does dyeing work? Where do the colors come from?
A: The colors come from chemical compounds called pigments. All plants (except a few rare albinos) produce many kinds of pigments, but except for chlorophyll—the green pigment responsible for photosynthesis—botanists really don't know much about pigments. A century ago, chemists catalogued hundreds of plant pigments, assigned them names, identified their molecular structures, and listed one or more plants where each pigment could be found. That's a start, but knowing names and structures doesn't begin to explain why plants make pigments, or what functions pigments might serve in a living plant, or why you sometimes find the same pigment in totally unrelated plants—but not necessarily in different species of the same genus. We simply don't know why some pigments are good for dyeing when most of them aren't, or what happens to pigments when you freeze or dry or boil the plants, or why some pigments dye wool but not cotton or vice versa, or how using different mordants can sometimes change the colors you get from a single pigment. I could go on and on—this stuff fascinates me—but I'd better get back to answering questions, not asking them.

Q: How much pigment does one dye plant produce?
A: Very little. The pigment only constitutes a few percent of the overall dry weight of a dye plant.

Q: Do some dye plants produce more pigment than others?
A: Yes. For example, woad and indigo yield the same blue dye, but indigo is more productive than woad. If you grew a dozen of each plant side by side in a garden, the indigo would produce enough pigment to dye several times as much wool as you could dye with the woad.

I'm sure that pigment yield also varies within a single species of dye plant. For example, it seems inevitable that some individual indigo plants produce more pigment than others do. All plants show that kind of variation. Just as horticulturists have selected and named countless strains of vegetables and flowers for their superior flavor, color, size, yield, vigor, etc., it should be possible to select and breed a special high-yielding strain of indigo or any other dye plant, but as far as I know, this has never been done. If you know a graduate student in horticulture who's looking for a research project, there's an idea.

One

CHOOSING WHICH PLANTS TO GROW

Gardeners never have enough time or space to grow all the plants that catch their interest. Even in the specialized realm of dye plants, there are scores of species to choose from, so it's challenging to decide which ones you really want and which ones you can live without. Fortunately, many excellent dye plants are annuals or fast-growing perennials; it only takes one growing season to decide whether to keep them or try something else. My dye garden is never the same from year to year because I'm always adding and subtracting plants as my enthusiasms for them wax and wane. In general, though, I follow certain guidelines in choosing plants for a dye garden, and here they are:

✦ Grow any plants that give good reds or blues because these colors are virtually unobtainable from uncultivated dye plants. Examples: madder, yellow bedstraw, indigo, Japanese indigo, and woad.

✦ Grow plants that give other interesting (that is, not just gold or tan) colors such as green, purple, or black. Examples: hibiscus, hollyhock, purple loosestrife, St.-John's-wort.

✦ Grow plants with such pretty flowers that you'd want them in the garden anyway, which also happen to produce good colors in the dyepot. Examples: dahlia, black-eyed Susan, zinnia.

✦ Grow herbs with such pleasant aromas that you'd want them in the garden anyway, which also happen to produce good colors in the dyepot. Examples: marjoram, bronze fennel, purple basil.

✦ Grow plants that are cheap, prolific, and easy so that you won't mind chopping them off in midseason and dumping them into a dyepot. (A precious, rare, or slow-growing plant may be a prize in the garden, but who could bear to harvest it?) Examples of cheap, easy plants: marigolds, yellow cosmos, tansy.

✦ Grow any seeds or plants that were passed along with the recommendation of a fellow gardener or dyer. (Continue the chain by sharing your favorite plants, too.)

THE PLANTS IN THIS BOOK

This book features thirty herbaceous plants—annuals, biennials, and perennials—that are easy to grow and are productive. I've chosen them because I think they're valuable in the dyepot, attractive in the garden, and/or interesting to work with. Most of these plants can be grown in any part of the continental United States if they are protected from extreme cold or heat and watered during dry spells. Some are common garden plants available at any garden center or nursery. Others are grown just for dyeing, and you'll have to order them by mail.

Along with the main plant that's featured in each entry, I've discussed closely related plants that you're likely to find in catalogs or at nurseries to help you choose good substitutes and avoid disappointments. As noted in each case, sometimes closely related species have equivalent dye potential, and sometimes they do not.

CONSIDER THE POTENTIAL YIELD

Vegetable growers know that different crops yield different amounts. A 10-foot row of beans provides many more meals than a 10-foot row of peas; one hill of zucchini makes too many squash, but one hill of cantaloupes only bears a few melons. Similarly, different dye plants yield more or less dye; a 10-foot row of dyer's coreopsis will dye several times as much yarn to a much darker color than a 10-foot row of zinnias. Yield is something to think about if your garden space is limited and you want to dye as much yarn as possible. Per square foot of garden space, some of the most efficient dye plants are broom sedge, coreopsis, dyer's coreopsis, garland chrysanthemum, indigo, marigold, and weld. By comparison, black-eyed Susan, hollyhock, purple loosestrife, St.-John's-wort, and sunflower fill a lot of garden space for the amount of dye they yield.

Don't worry about yield if you just want to experiment with a variety of dye plants and make lots of sample skeins that you can combine in a multicolored project. However, if you want to dye enough yarn in one color to knit a sweater or weave an afghan, it's a good idea to plan ahead and make sure you grow enough plants to dye all the yarn you need. For more information on yield, check the individual plant entries and the chart on page 31.

DYE PLANTS NOT TO GROW

Some dye plants aren't worth growing. For example, common weeds such as bindweed, cocklebur, ragweed, redroot pigweed, and dock give attractive shades of gold, tan, orange, olive green, and brown, but they are so abundant and so unloved that you can gather all you want along roadsides or from vacant lots without a twinge of selfishness. Most people will think you're crazy to want them. You *would* be crazy to grow them.

Several trees and shrubs yield good dyes, but few of these are good garden plants. The black walnut tree is well known to dyers because its nut hulls are unequaled for rich brown dyes. The fallen nuts are very messy, though, and a single tree bears far more than you can use. The leaves and twigs from willows, poplars, and cottonwoods give bright yellows and golds, but the trees have brittle wood that breaks in storms and thirsty roots that invade sewer and water pipes. Barberry roots give a good yellow, but you have to dig up the shrub to get the roots. Osage orange wood gives excellent yellows and golds, but you have to cut off limbs or fell the tree to get the wood. Actually, if you had an osage orange tree, you might *want* to fell the darned thing; it is quite thorny and drops bushels of big sticky fruit-balls that repel cockroaches but aren't good for much else. If you have a lot of space for a shrub and it doesn't grow wild in your neighborhood, you might consider staghorn sumac (*Rhus typhina*) or any of the other shrubby sumacs. Although they may spread by suckering, they're all easy to grow and have bright fall foliage. In the dyepot, sumacs are desirable not for their bright red berries, which only give a rosy beige dye, but for their tannin-rich leaves, which are useful for mordanting cotton.

Like sumac berries, the berries from elderberries, mulberries, blackberries and other fruit crops make luscious-colored dyebaths, but nearly all berry-dyed colors fade away when exposed to light. Over a period of months or years, even the dim light from a north window will erase the pinks and purples of berry-dyed yarn, leaving only tans. I grow several kinds of berries, but I don't dye with them anymore. I just eat them or watch the birds eat them.

I wouldn't grow them specifically for dyeing, but the unused parts of some vegetable plants give good colors. Carrot tops give a warm yellow, and onion skins give brassy golds. On the other hand, beets or red cabbage don't make the purple colors you'd expect, and the colors they do produce are neither attractive nor permanent.

Finally, here are a few more plants that I don't recommend for a dye garden. Even though they're included in most dye books, safflower, saffron, alkanet, and bloodroot all have drawbacks. Picking safflower (*Carthamus tinctoria*) blossoms is tiresome because the plants are so prickly, and besides, safflower dyes fade quickly. Saffron (*Crocus sativus*) is far too expensive and scarce to use for dyeing yarn, especially when so many other plants give equivalent yellows and golds. It's virtually impossible to find seeds or plants of the true alkanet (*Alkanna tinctoria*), and the dried, imported alkanet roots that you can buy make odd colors that fade fast. Bloodroot (*Sanguinaria canadensis*), a lovely perennial woodland wildflower, grows too slowly to sacrifice for colors that you could easily get from the annual dyer's coreopsis. Furthermore, dust from bloodroot-dyed yarn can irritate your respiratory system.

Two

GETTING AND GROWING DYE PLANTS

When you've decided which plants you want to include in your dye garden, make a list and start researching where to obtain each plant. In the "How to grow" section of each entry in this book, I've indicated whether the plant is easy or hard to find, whether it's available at local nurseries and garden centers or only by mail order, and whether it's sold as seeds or as plants.

The easiest way to fill a dye garden is to choose plants that you can buy as transplants at a local nursery in spring. Just bring home a carload of coreopsis, dahlias, black-eyed Susan, yarrow, marigolds, zinnias, dyer's chamomile, and hardy hibiscus, and you'll have the potential to make lots of colors.

However, some of the best dye plants are available only by mail, often only as seeds. I didn't name particular mail-order suppliers for each plant in this book because many nurseries change their catalog listings from year to year. If you need to order seeds by mail, plan ahead and request several catalogs in December or early January. That way, you can study the current catalogs, find what you're looking for, and place your orders before the suppliers get too busy for prompt turnaround. If anything you ordered is out of stock, you'll still have time to order it from a different supplier, and you'll be ready to start seeds in late winter or early spring, as appropriate. If you're ordering plants by mail, send in your order as soon as you've decided what you want, and specify when you want them delivered—usually about the time of your last spring frost. Most nurseries stop shipping live plants during the hot summer months, but they do ship again in the fall if you want to expand your garden then.

GROWING DYE PLANTS FROM SEEDS

Raising plants from seeds is very satisfying, and it's a thrifty and efficient way to fill a garden. Many of the plants in this book grow so quickly that you can start dyeing within 3 to 6 months of sowing the seeds. The two main methods, described below, are sowing the seeds indoors and transplanting seedlings into the garden or sowing the seeds directly where you want the plants to grow.

Raising seedlings indoors

Sowing seeds indoors is a good idea if you have a short growing season (less than 120 frost-free days). You can get a significant head start by sowing seeds 6 to 10 weeks before the last frost. This is especially helpful for perennials such as dyer's chamomile, yarrow, and hardy hibiscus, all of which can bloom the first year if started early enough. Sowing indoors is also recommended for seeds that are rare, expensive, or very small because you have more control over the growing conditions indoors, where you can protect the seeds and seedlings from extreme temperatures, downpours and droughts, hungry birds, and wayward pets.

If you've ever grown your own seedlings of tomatoes, peppers, or other garden plants, the same techniques apply to dye plants. If you haven't grown seedlings indoors before, here are the basics. For best results, I recommend growing seedlings under fluorescent lights, not on a windowsill; windowsills are too hot and dry in the daytime, too cold and drafty at night, and too dark on cloudy days. For less than $20, you can buy a fluorescent shop-light fixture and an automatic timer (set it to turn the lights on at 6 a.m. and off at midnight). Hang the fixture from the ceiling or improvise a frame to

DYE PLANTS THAT YOU CAN HARVEST
THE FIRST YEAR FROM SEED

Starting from seed is the most economical way to plant a dye garden, and the dye plants listed here grow so fast that you can start dyeing yarn only 3 to 6 months after sowing the seeds. The letters before each plant name indicate the best way to sow the seeds. "D" means sow directly in the garden. "I" means sow the seeds indoors. "D, I" means sow indoors or out, as you choose.

D	Black-eyed Susan (*choose the "Gloriosa daisy" type*)	D, I	Marigolds
D, I	Bronze fennel	I	Marjoram
I	Broom sedge	D	Peppergrass
I	Coreposis (*choose an early strain*)	D, I	Purple basil (*wait until the soil is warm*)
D, I	Dahlia	I	Purple loosestrife
D	Dyer's coreopsis	D	Sunflower
I	Dyer's chamomile	I	Tansy
D	Garland chrysanthemum	D	Weld
I	Hardy hibiscus	D	Woad
D, I	Hollyhock (*choose an annual strain*)	I	Yarrow
D	Hop (*choose the annual hop*)	D, I	Yellow cosmos
D, I	Indigo (*wait until the soil is warm*)	D, I	Zinnia
I	Japanese indigo		

support it over the seedlings. Adjust its position as they grow, keeping the tubes 3 to 4 inches above the leaves.

Buy a bag of sterile seed-starting mix at any garden center. Gather some shallow plastic pots, such as the six-packs that nurseries use for seedlings, other small nursery pots, or yogurt cups with holes punched in the bottom. If you're using recycled containers, wash them well in hot soapy water with a little bleach added. Pour some of the soil mix into a plastic dishpan, stir in enough warm water to moisten and then wait an hour or so for the water to be absorbed. Spoon the moist soil into the containers, filling them to within 1/2 inch of the top.

With a pencil, poke very shallow holes in the soil and sow one or more seeds in each pot, dropping the seeds into the holes. With your fingers, gently pat the soil to fill in the holes and level the surface. Set the pots in a waterproof flat or tray and put it under the lights. At 70° F, seedlings of most plants discussed in this book will germinate in 1 to 3 weeks. If your house is cooler than that, find a warm place on top of the TV, next to the water heater, over a heat vent, etc. Put the pots there just until the seeds germinate, then immediately move them under the lights.

After sowing seeds, check the pots once or twice a day to see whether the soil is beginning to dry out and to watch for emerging sprouts. Drying out is fatal, and it's important to move the seedlings into bright light as soon as they sprout; otherwise, they'll stretch out thin and tall and get very weak. Position the fluorescent tubes within 3 to 4 inches of the seedlings' leaves.

As they grow, water the seedlings whenever the top of the soil dries out, and fertilize once a week with any soluble house plant fertilizer diluted to half the recommended strength. If you sowed more than one seed per pot, choose the strongest seedling to save and snip off the others with sharp scissors.

Continue watering and fertilizing the seedlings, raising the lights as they grow, until the weather gets mild. Then start preparing them for life in the garden. At first, set the pots outdoors in a shady, protected area. Each day, expose them to more sun and wind. At this stage, the pots dry out quickly, so water them thoroughly at least once a day. After several days, as soon as the seedlings are tough enough not to wilt in the sun and wind, go ahead and transplant them into the ground.

Sowing seeds in the garden

Sowing into the ground, or direct seeding, is good for plants that grow quickly from seed and for plants with fragile roots that can be damaged by transplanting. Some gardeners sow most of their seeds directly, convinced that the resulting plants are stronger and more attractive. Direct seeding is risky, though, if you have erratic weather or a limited supply of seeds. I start most of my seeds indoors, and only direct-sow common, cheap, fast-growing plants such as sunflowers, marigolds, zinnias, dyer's coreopsis, weld, and woad.

First, dig or till and rake the soil. The soil should be just moist. Then decide where you want plants to grow, measuring with a yardstick to ensure enough space between plants, and place a marker or plant label at each planting site. Sow a few seeds at each site, cover them with a thin layer (about twice the thickness of the seeds) of soil, and top with a scattering of pine needles or grass clippings to keep the soil from drying out too fast. Check the marked sites daily and sprinkle with water if the soil looks dry. When the seedlings are a few inches tall, choose the one that looks most vigorous and pinch off or pull out the others.

Saving seeds

You can grow many dye plants from seeds that you save, and saving your own seeds has several advantages. It's a way to save money, and it also saves you the time and trouble of looking through catalogs and placing new orders every year. This is especially worthwhile if you want to grow garland chrysanthemum, peppergrass, indigo, or Japanese indigo—all desirable dye plants which, for some reason, are listed in few seed catalogs. It's also worth saving seeds from more common plants such as dyer's coreopsis, dark-colored hollyhocks, bronze fennel, weld, and woad. If you don't need them yourself, you can share them with other dyers.

Although certain kinds of plants are self-pollinating and so a single plant of a given variety may set seed, usually cross-pollination between two or more individuals of the same kind of plant increases the seed set. When the flowers fade, watch for developing seed heads or pods, and keep a close eye as they swell, change color, dry out, and/or harden. Let the seeds ripen as long as possible on the plant, but pick them before they scatter on the ground and are lost. Pick whole pods or seed heads, put them in a paper bag or shallow box (labeled), and set it in a warm airy place to dry. After a week or so, separate the seeds from any hulls or debris, put them in a paper packet labeled with the plant name and the year, and store the packet in a cool, dry place. I keep my seeds in the refrigerator sealed in a plastic container with an airtight lid.

PERENNIAL DYE PLANTS
THAT YOU CAN
PROPAGATE BY DIVISION

Black-eyed Susan
Broomsedge, little bluestem
Coreopsis
Dahlia (save the tubers)
Dyer's chamomile
Goldenrod
Madder
Purple loosestrife
St.-John's-Wort
Tansy
Yarrow
Yellow bedstraw

PROPAGATING PERENNIAL DYE PLANTS BY DIVISION

Several of the perennial dye plants can be propagated by division, that is, by cutting or pulling a plant apart and replanting the separate portions. It's best to do this in early spring just as the new shoots are starting to expand or in the fall after the plant has finished flowering. Start by digging straight down around the plant 6 to 8 inches from the stems, then angle the shovel underneath the roots and try to lift up. You may be surprised at how deep the roots go and how much soil sticks to them, and how hard it is to lift that mass out of the hole. Next, try to shake or knock off enough soil that you

can see how the roots and shoots are connected. Look for new shoots or shoot buds, and break or cut the plant into sections that each have a few shoots or buds and the roots that go with them. It's better to have a few big strong divisions than a lot of little weak ones. Discard any tough old roots that don't have any shoots or buds. Replant the divisions promptly into freshly prepared soil, and water well. Keep watch over the new plants for the next several weeks, and water again whenever the soil gets dry.

One reason for making divisions is to increase your stock of dye plants that don't come true from seed or grow slowly from seed. For example, you can buy one pot of 'Morden Pink' loosestrife, grow it for a year or two, then dig it up and divide it into four to six or more new plants. If you're patient, that's an economical way to fill or expand a dye garden. Another reason for dividing a plant is to renew its vigor. After growing in the same spot for a few years, a clump of goldenrod often dies out in the center. Dig it up, save portions from the healthy outer edge to replant, and discard the middle. Finally, dividing and replanting is a way to limit a plant's spread. Tansy sends underground runners that soon fill a bed if you let it. To prevent that, dig up the tansy patch every year or two, keep a few healthy chunks to replant, and discard the rest.

CONTROLLING INVASIVE OR WEEDY DYE PLANTS

Six of the plants in this book—fennel, yellow bedstraw, purple loosestrife, St.-John's-wort, tansy, and woad—are European natives that have spread like weeds in parts of this country. Weeds provoke strong emotions, and some people view these and other foreign weeds as a threat to the environment. I think weeds are a minor worry compared with acid rain, toxic waste, and other issues of our day, but I do advise you to be a responsible gardener. First, learn and follow the laws of your state. If a plant is banned, don't grow it. Second, if a plant is weedy in your neighborhood, don't think about growing it yourself. Ask permission from the landowner and explain your interest, and I'm sure you'll be able to collect more than you can use. Third, if a plant is not weedy in your area, go ahead and grow in in your garden, but guard against its spread. Harvest and use or destroy the flower stalks before seeds ripen and scatter.

Some of the other dye plants in this book, while not weed problems on a regional scale, can be invasive within the context of a small garden because they spread by underground runners or produce lots of volunteer seedlings. This isn't necessarily a problem—you can toss the extra plants in the dyepot or give them away—but just in case, the individual entries warn you about plants with expansionist tendencies.

· *Three* ·

PLANNING A DYE GARDEN

You don't need to make a special garden for dye plants. You can simply devote a few rows of your vegetable garden to dye crops or include some dye plants in a flower bed or border. But making a special dye garden is fun, and it's an interesting project to share with your gardening and fibercraft friends. Whether it's small or large, planning, tending, and harvesting a dye garden is a satisfying experience that gives you a lasting souvenir: a basket full of beautiful colored yarn.

GARDEN BASICS

Choose a site that gets full sun for at least six hours a day during the growing season or, better yet, full sun all day. Few dye plants grow well in the shade.

The garden can be round, square, oblong, or whatever shape you like, and it can be small or large, depending on how much space you have and how much time you have to care for the garden and do the dyeing. For your first dye garden, however, I recommend starting small and keeping it simple so that you can stay on top of the gardening work and have enough time for dyeing, too.

Use stakes and string and a measuring tape or yardstick to mark the outlines of the planting beds. You'll need to be able to reach every plant, to care for it as it grows, and to gather its leaves and/or flowers for dyeing. Most people can reach into the center of a bed up to 4 or 5 feet in diameter, but if you find that uncomfortable, make the bed narrower, arrange the plants in rows (as in a vegetable garden), or build raised beds to bring the plants up closer to you. Making raised beds involves some extra effort and expense—you'll need to build an edging of landscape timbers, boards, stones, bricks, or blocks, and to bring in enough soil to fill the bed—but your effort will be rewarded by improved plant growth and by easier picking.

Prepare the soil as you would for a vegetable garden or flower bed. Remove the sod or existing plants, then dig deeply to loosen the soil and remove any rocks, debris, or roots. Work in some compost, aged manure, peat moss, or other organic matter to improve drainage and help retain water and nutrients. (Several dye plants tolerate poor soil, but they get larger and give more dye if you grow them in good soil.)

If the bed is surrounded by lawn, it's a good idea to install an edging of some kind to keep the grass out of the planting area, or to remove enough sod to make a path at least 2 feet wide around the edge of each bed and between adjacent beds. Topping it with a layer of wood chips, pine needles, or other mulch will help keep weeds from growing in the path and dirt off your shoes.

PLAN THE GARDEN ON PAPER FIRST

Take time to consider different options on paper. Sketching possible planting arrangements helps you decide which plants to put where and how many of each you can grow. Without a plan, most gardeners are tempted to set too many plants too close together because in early spring the plants look so small and the empty bed looks so big.

I've provided four sample plans in this book, but you can easily design your own. To sketch a plan, measure the dimensions of the bed(s) in your planned dye garden, then draw the shape(s) on paper. Choose a simple scale, such as 1/2 inch on the plan equals 1 foot in the garden, or 1 square on graph paper equals 1 square foot in the garden. I find it easiest to think of spacing and yield in terms of square feet, and using graph paper makes this kind of planning easier. Refer to the chart on page 31 to see how much space each plant needs, then fill in the appropriate number of squares on the plan, or mark an area on the plan that you'd like to fill with a certain kind of plant and then refer to the chart to see how many individual plants will fit there.

At the same time as you're considering how many of each plant to put in the garden, you can be thinking about how to arrange them—short ones in front or around the edge, tall ones in back or in the center, etc. You might alternate the plain green plants such as broom sedge and indigo with showy-flowered plants such as cosmos and dahlias. I usually keep annuals and perennials separate so that I can replant the annuals next year without disturbing the perennials, but you can intersperse them if you choose.

Sketching plans like this is a pleasant way to spend a rainy afternoon or winter evening. You'll use up several sheets of paper, but when you're done, you'll have figured out a way to make your dye garden as productive and attractive as possible. Follow the plan as you're planting; later, you can refer to it to identify which plant is which if you're not familiar with them yet. Use labels to mark each plant, too, to help you keep track of what's where. Make notes throughout the season on how the different plants grew, how big they got, and how satisfied you were with the dyes they gave. Then save the notes with the plan so you can rearrange and refine the garden in future years.

A DAISY-SHAPED BED OF COMPOSITE FLOWERS

This little round flower bed, 5 feet in diameter, mimics the shape of the flowers it contains. All seven of these dye plants belong to the Compositae, or daisy family, and have rounded or daisy-shaped blossoms. I put the garland chrysanthemum in the center, because it grows the tallest. Choose dwarf types of the other flowers to fill in around the edge. You can raise all these plants from seeds, which are listed in many garden-seed catalogs. If your growing season is short and you want a head start, sow the seeds indoors 6 weeks before the last frost. Otherwise, you can sow them all directly into the garden as soon as the soil is warm. If you pick the faded flowers every few days, the plants will keep blooming all summer. Save the flowers in plastic bags (one for each kind of flower) in the freezer, and you'll end up with enough to dye several ounces— perhaps even a pound—of wool. If you want to dye even more yarn, omit the zinnias and substitute extra dyer's coreopsis or French marigolds.

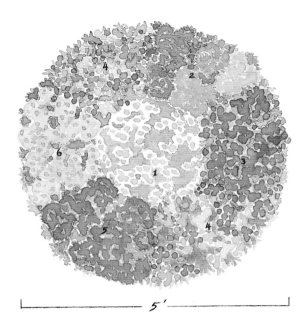

DAISY-SHAPED BED

*Planting key: The number in parentheses tells how many of each
plant to put in the colored area.*

1. Garland chrysanthemum (3)
2. Dwarf dahlia (3)
3. Yellow cosmos (6)
4. Zinnia (3 + 3)
5. French marigold (3)
6. Dyer's coreopsis (6)

A RAISED-BED DYE GARDEN

This rectangular garden, 5 feet wide by 12 feet long is designed to be viewed from both sides. It could be planted at ground level, but putting it in a raised bed brings the plants up closer to you for easier picking. Aside from convenience, a raised bed is also an attractive feature for a garden—it's like setting the plants on a stage. You can use landscape timbers, old railroad ties, 2 × 8 boards, or concrete blocks for the edges of the bed. Fill it with a mixture of your best topsoil and plenty of compost, aged manure, or peat moss.

The hardy hibiscus in the center of the bed is a reliable perennial that will come back year after year but won't spread to take over the bed. Everything else, including the bronze fennel, can be grown as an annual. If your last frost comes after April 15, I'd recommend starting the hibiscus, fennel, indigo, Japanese indigo, marjoram, dwarf dahlias, and purple basil indoors. After frost, when the soil is warm, you can transplant these seedlings and direct-sow the other plants. If your last frost comes earlier than that, you can direct-sow everything if you choose.

If you pick flowers and leaves regularly and dye successive batches of yarn throughout the summer and early fall, you'll be able to dye about 2 pounds of wool yarn from this garden.

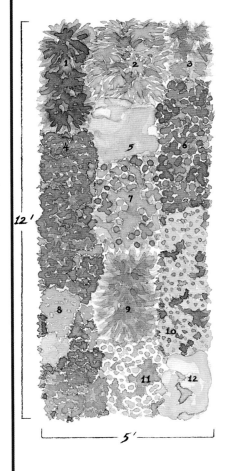

RAISED-BED GARDEN

Planting key: The number in parentheses tells how many of each plant to put in the colored area.

1. Purple basil (5)
2. Japanese indigo (3)
3. Weld (3)
4. French marigolds (5)
5. Bronze fennel (3)
6. Yellow cosmos (12)
7. Hardy hibiscus (1)
8. Dwarf dahlias (5)
9. Indigo (5)
10. Dyer's coreopsis (12)
11. Garland chrysanthemum (3)
12. Marjoram (3)

A MIXED-BORDER DYE GARDEN

Like many flower gardens, this dye garden includes a mixture of annuals, biennials, and perennials to provide a sequence of bloom from midspring (if you let the woad overwinter and blossom) through fall. You could site it along a property line or on the south or east side of a fence, wall, or hedge (if planting next to a hedge, leave a few feet of open space in between, to avoid damaging the hedge plants' roots). The dimensions are 6 feet wide by 20 feet long. I've put the taller (mostly perennial) dye plants along the back and the shorter (all annual or biennial) dye plants in front, leaving space for a foot-wide access path so that you can step into the garden and move along between the plants for picking and weeding. You might want to lay stepping stones along this path, or if you have plenty of room, make the garden 7 feet wide with a 2-foot path.

You'll need to order some of these plants and several kinds of seeds by mail, but you should be able to find some of the perennials and annual flowers at local garden centers. Bury an old board on edge between the yellow bedstraw and purple loosestrife to keep their roots separate, and wait until the second or third year after planting before digging the yellow bedstraw roots. Leaves, flowers, and tops from the other plants will fill many dyepots throughout the summer and fall—enough to dye about 2 pounds of wool in a wide variety of colors.

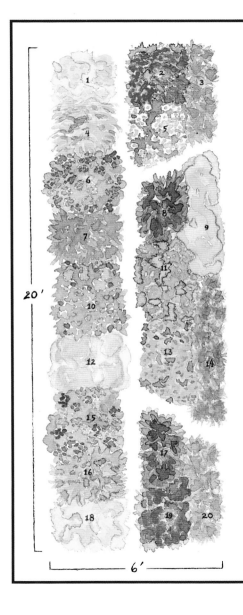

MIXED-BORDER GARDEN

Planting key: The number in parentheses tells how many of each plant to put in the colored area.

1. Curly tansy (1)
2. French marigold (3)
3. Woad (6)
4. Goldenrod (1)
5. Garland chrysanthemum (3)
6. Hollyhock (1)
7. Indigo (3)
8. Purple basil (5)
9. Marjoram (8)
10. Hardy hibiscus (1)
11. Dahlia (3)
12. Bronze fennel (1)
13. Dyer's coreopsis (10)
14. Weld (8)
15. Hollyhock (1)
16. Purple loosestrife (2)
17. Purple basil (5)
18. Yellow bedstraw (1)
19. Yellow cosmos (10)
20. Woad (6)

A PRODUCTION GARDEN

This garden is organized like a vegetable garden, not a flower bed, to simplify caring for and harvesting a larger number of dye plants. It has eight beds, each 4 feet wide and 8 feet long, separated and surrounded by paths for a total area of 23 feet wide and 26 feet long. The beds may be level with the ground or raised, depending on your soil conditions and preference. Four of the beds contain perennial dye plants that may be left in place for a few years at a time. The other four are replanted each year.

If you use plenty of mulch on the paths and around the plants to control weeds and keep the soil moist, the main activity in tending a large dye garden is keeping up with the harvest. You could spend a few hours every week from midsummer through fall dyeing successive batches of yarn in dozens of different colors. By the end of the growing season, this garden could produce enough plant material to dye about 7 pounds of wool yarn—enough for several sweaters or a couple of blankets or rugs. Designing, planting, tending, and using a garden of this size or larger would be a good project for a spinning guild or herb society, and you could dye enough yarn that everyone would end up with samples to save as well as skeins to use.

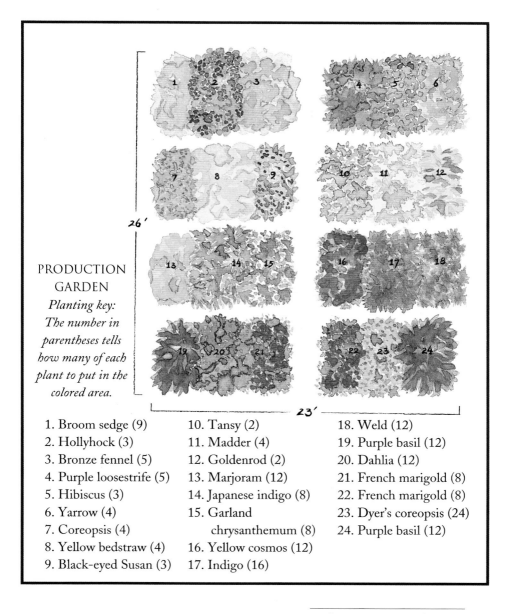

26'

PRODUCTION
GARDEN

*Planting key:
The number in
parentheses tells
how many of each
plant to put in the
colored area.*

23'

1. Broom sedge (9)
2. Hollyhock (3)
3. Bronze fennel (5)
4. Purple loosestrife (5)
5. Hibiscus (3)
6. Yarrow (4)
7. Coreopsis (4)
8. Yellow bedstraw (4)
9. Black-eyed Susan (3)

10. Tansy (2)
11. Madder (4)
12. Goldenrod (2)
13. Marjoram (12)
14. Japanese indigo (8)
15. Garland
    chrysanthemum (8)
16. Yellow cosmos (12)
17. Indigo (16)

18. Weld (12)
19. Purple basil (12)
20. Dahlia (12)
21. French marigold (8)
22. French marigold (8)
23. Dyer's coreopsis (24)
24. Purple basil (12)

SPACING AND YIELD OF DYE PLANTS

Here are some numbers to help you decide how many plants you can fit into your garden and how many individuals of any particular dye plant you will need to dye 4 ounces of wool yarn—enough to knit a hat or a pair of mittens. The numbers are approximate, and are based on my experience. Your own yield may vary, depending on the quality of your soil, the length of your growing season, how often you harvest material for dyeing, and whether you prefer dark or pale colors on your yarn.

The number in the first column tells how much space the plants need, measured in square feet. For the perennials, this is enough space for the first two years; after that, they may need more space or have to be divided.

The number in the second column tells how many plants are needed to dye 4 ounces of wool yarn to a medium or dark shade. I don't have enough data to give specific figures for silk or cotton, but in general, you need more plants to dye these fibers than to dye wool. You may be able to dye more yarn in paler colors. With some plants, such as purple loosestrife or broom sedge, you can gather whole plant tops and dye the 4 ounces of yarn all at once. With flowers such as cosmos or dahlias, you'll need to pick regularly and dye several smaller batches of yarn, or save up the flowers until you can dye the yarn all at once at the end of the growing season. You'll also need to do successive batches of indigo, dyer's indigo, or woad. For madder and yellow bedstraw, you have to wait at least two or three years before you can dig the roots and dye the 4 ounces of yarn.

The number in the third column tells how many square feet of garden space is required to grow enough of that plant to dye 4 ounces of yarn. This is the "bottom line" number to look at if you're interested in comparing the yield of different plants.

SPACING AND YIELD OF DYE PLANTS

Suggested spacing in sq. ft.	# of plants to dye 4 oz. wool	Sq. ft. needed to dye 4 oz.	Plant name
4 sq.ft./plant	12	48	Black-eyed Susan
2 sq.ft/plant	8	16	Bronze fennel
1 sq.ft./plant	6	6	Broom sedge
2 sq.ft./plant	2–3	4–6	Coreopsis
1–4 sq.ft./plant	4–8	12	Dahlia
2 sq.ft./plant	12	24	Dyer's chamomile
2 plants/sq.ft.	6–8	3–4	Dyer's coreopsis
4 sq.ft./plant	4	16	Dyer's greenweed
1 sq.ft./plant	4–6	4–6	Garland chrysanthemum
4 sq.ft./plant	4	16	Goldenrod
4 sq.ft./plant	4	16	Hardy hibiscus
4 sq.ft./plant	8–12	32–48	Hollyhock
4 sq.ft./plant	2	8	Hop
1 sq.ft./plant	2–4	2–4	Indigo
2 sq.ft./plant	2–4	4–8	Japanese indigo
4 sq.ft./plant	2	8	Madder
1 sq.ft./plant	4–6	4–6	Marigolds
2 plants/sq.ft.	24	12	Marjoram
4 plants/sq.ft.	24–32	6–8	Peppergrass
1 sq.ft./plant	18	18	Purple basil
2 sq.ft./plant	18	36	Purple loosestrife
2 sq.ft./plant	24	48	St.-John's-wort
2–4 sq.ft./plant	12	24–48	Sunflower
4 sq.ft./plant	4	16	Tansy
2 plants/sq.ft.	6–12	3–6	Weld
1 sq.ft./plant	24	24	Woad
2 sq.ft./plant	12	24	Yarrow
4 sq.ft./plant	4	16	Yellow bedstraw
2 plants/sq.ft.	12	6	Yellow cosmos
1 sq.ft./plant	16–24	16–24	Zinnia

Four

The Basics of Dyeing With Plants

D yeing is a lot like cooking—it involves measuring, simmering, adjusting the burner, watching the timer, and awaiting the results with a mixture of optimism and uncertainty. And just as different cooks have their own recipes, techniques, and shortcuts, different dyers have their own methods and motives. Here is my favorite approach, which breaks the process into three separate steps: preparing and mordanting the yarn, gathering plants and making a dyebath, and dyeing the yarn. I use the same procedure for all of the dye plants mentioned in this book except indigo, Japanese indigo, and woad. They require a different method, which is described at the end of this chapter.

EQUIPMENT AND FACILITIES FOR DYEING

You can find all the tools you'll need for dyeing at a hardware or discount store. Just don't borrow tools from your kitchen. Put together a special set of dye equipment, label each tool as a dyeing tool, and keep the equipment separate from your cooking supplies. You'll need:

✦ One or more pots large enough to hold 3 to 5 gallons of water. Enamel canning kettles or stainless steel stockpots are often recommended, but aluminum pots may be used, too. Each pot should have a lid.

✦ Plastic tubs or buckets, some with lids, for soaking yarn and storing fluids.

✦ Wooden rods or a long-handled spoon or barbecue fork for stirring dyebaths and handling yarn.

✦ A wire mesh strainer.

✦ Rubber gloves.

✦ A candy, dairy, or scientific thermometer.

✦ A set of measuring spoons for measuring mordants.

✦ Scales for weighing fibers and dye plants. A laboratory balance that's calibrated in grams is most accurate, but you may use a postal or diet scale that weighs in ounces.

✦ A camp stove, portable electric burner, or other heat source. Set it on a table or bench that is fairly low because you'll be lifting heavy dyepots back and forth.

✦ A well-ventilated workplace. Working outdoors or in a breezy porch or shed is usually best. Dyeing is too smelly and messy and makes too much clutter to do in the kitchen, and you may be tempted to use kitchen pots and pans to dye with.

✦ Access to a sink or tap. You'll need plenty of water for soaking, dyeing, washing, and rinsing.

CHOOSING AND PREPARING YARN FOR DYEING

Plant dyes are versatile. I usually dye wool fleece that I plan to spin or skeins of yarn that I've already spun from wool, silk, cotton, and other natural fibers, but I know other people who use plant dyes to dye lengths of fabric, finished garments, leather, wood, paper, reeds and stems for basketry, Easter eggs, candles, even fur and feathers for tying fishing flies. It takes some experimentation to develop suitable techniques for dyeing different materials, but the results can be lovely in every case.

If you're new to dyeing, I recommend that you start with pure wool yarn in its natural or plain white color. You can buy it at most knitting or weaving stores, at sheep and wool festivals, or from the mail-order suppliers that advertise in *Spin·Off*, *Handwoven, Knitter's, Threads,* and similar magazines. Wind the yarn into skeins about one yard in circumference. For sampling many colors, I like to make small skeins that weigh 1/2 ounce or less. If you want to dye a lot of yarn the same color, make larger skeins, up to 4 ounces. Tie the two ends of the yarn together in a bow or knot, leaving tails a few inches long, and tie three or four pieces of white cotton string in loops around the skein to keep it from tangling.The yarn must be clean, so remove oils or finishes by washing it in warm water and liquid dishwashing detergent. Then rinse it in warm clear water.

After you've had some experience in dyeing with wool, try dyeing yarn made from other fibers. Mohair, alpaca, angora, dog fur, and other fibers from animals—called protein fibers—behave like wool in the dyepot, resulting in similar colors. Silk is a protein fiber, too, but it doesn't necessarily mimic wool and often picks up different colors.

Cotton, flax, ramie, and other fibers from plants are cellulose fibers. Cellulose fibers dye well with plant dyes, but they often need more concentrated dyebaths and longer simmering and soaking than protein fibers. If put in the same dyebath, protein and cellulose fibers usually absorb different colors.

MORDANTING

Most plant dyes work best if the yarn is mordanted, or treated with a small amount of a metallic compound. This makes the dye colors brighter and less likely to fade. The most com-

THE MOST COMMON MORDANTS

Aluminum. The aluminum compound used for mordanting is alum (potassium aluminum sulfate), a white powder that's also used in deodorants and foot powders and as a soil acidifier for hydrangeas and broad-leaved evergreens. Another form of alum (ammonium aluminum sulfate) is used in making pickles. Alum gives good results with most dye plants and is the most commonly used mordant. To mordant wool, silk, and other protein fibers, the alum is applied in combination with cream of tartar (potassium acid tartrate). For cotton and other cellulose fibers, the alum is applied alternately with tannic acid. Using too much alum on wool gives it a sticky feeling that won't wash out, but this doesn't happen to other fibers. Dyeing in aluminum pots has some effect in brightening dye colors, but not enough aluminum dissolves to prevent fading.

Tin. The tin compound used for mordanting is stannous chloride, which occurs as white crystals. A similar but more expensive compound, stannous fluoride, is used in decay-preventive toothpastes. Tin brightens colors, particularly reds, oranges, and yellows, but too much tin makes wool or silk very brittle and fragile. To avoid this, some dyers use just a pinch of tin, added at the end of the dyeing, on wool premordanted with alum. Dyeing in tin cans (which are actually tin-plated steel cans) doesn't dissolve enough tin to be effective as a mordant. Tin is rarely used on cellulose fibers.

Iron. Dyers in ancient times used iron-rich mud or water as a mordant or simply simmered their dyebaths in iron pots. These methods are still effective, but modern dyers often use a green powder called iron sulfate or copperas

that's also sold as a soil conditioner for broad-leaved evergreens. Iron generally darkens colors, and when used with some plants it produces grays or blacks. Using too much iron makes any fiber brittle, but you can use a weak afterbath of iron on fiber premordanted with alum with good results.

Copper. As a mordant, copper is used like iron to darken the dye colors, but it is less harsh on the fibers than iron. The copper compound used for mordanting is copper sulfate, also called blue vitriol, which forms brilliant blue crystals. Copper sulfate is also used as in agricultural fungicides (organic gardeners consider copper products much safer than other fungicides), in wood preservatives, and to control root growth in sewers and algae in ponds. Dyeing in a copper pot or adding a copper scrubpad to the dyebath are other ways to achieve the darkening effect of copper.

Chrome. Potassium dichromate, an orange powder, is a chrome compound used to mordant wool and mohair, but it is rarely used for other fibers. It gives bright colors and makes the wool feel soft and silky. Chrome is getting a lot of attention these days as a nutritional supplement, but prolonged exposure to chrome compounds has been shown to cause allergies, respiratory problems, and even cancer. Some dyers prefer not to use chrome at all. I use it occasionally, but I handle it carefully, do all of my mordanting in just a few sessions per year, and treat the used solution as hazardous waste. Most dye books repeat a warning that chrome mordant solutions are sensitive to light, but that's an "old dyer's tale", and you can disregard it.

mon mordants are compounds of aluminum, tin, iron, copper, or chrome; they are usually sold in powder or crystal form (see page 35). Packets of mordants are available from mail-order dye suppliers. Treat mordants with the same precautions you use with bleach, oven cleaner, gasoline, fertilizer, and other chemical products. Keep them in labeled containers out of the reach of children, and wear rubber gloves when you're handling mordants or mordanted yarn.

It's possible to do mordanting and dyeing at the same time, but I prefer to do the steps separately. I mordant a big supply of yarn early in the summer during the slack season after I've planted the dye garden but before there's anything to pick, and so I have yarn ready to use when the dye plants are ready. Mordanting ahead of time is much more convenient than having to mordant some yarn each time you want to dye. It's especially handy to have sample-size skeins pretreated with different mordants. That way, when you're experimenting with new dye plants, you can try all the mordants at once, to see if they make different colors. They often do.

Mordanting protein fibers

Fill a big pot, allowing at least 4 gallons of water per pound of yarn. Weigh the yarn and put it in a basin of water to soak for an hour or so. Meanwhile, measure out the appropriate amount of mordant (see page 37). Dissolve the mordant in a glass jar of hot water, stirring until all the crystals disappear, then add it to the big pot and stir some more. Add the wet yarn, heat the water slowly to a simmer (180° to 200°F), and simmer it for an hour. Set the pot off the heat and let it cool for several hours or until it is lukewarm. Remove the yarn, wash and rinse it well, and dye it immediately or dry it to dye at a future date. Label each skein with the name of the mordant that you used. I cut labels from the plastic flagging tape that landscape contractors use to mark trees and write on them with a waterproof marker.

Mordanting cellulose fibers

Use alum and tannic acid, which you will apply in three steps. For one pound of yarn, prepare two solutions:

✦ Mix 1/2 cup of alum with 4 gallons of hot water.

✦ Make a tannic acid solution by simmering several ounces of sumac leaves in 4 gallons of water for one hour or by dissolving 2 tablespoons of tannic acid powder

MEASURING MORDANTS FOR WOOL, SILK, AND OTHER PROTEIN FIBERS

These three tables are designed for different situations, but they all provide approximately the same ratio of mordant to fiber and give similar results.

1. For large projects or group activities, it's practical to prepare yarn in 1-pound quantities. For 1 pound of clean dry yarn, measure your choice of mordant in the following amounts:

+ 4 tablespoons of alum plus
  4 teaspoons of cream of tartar
+ 2 teaspoons of tin
+ 2 tablespoons of copper
+ 2 tablespoons of iron
+ 3 teaspoons of chrome

2. For sampling and experimentation, it's better to have small batches of different yarns prepared with different mordants. To mordant 4 ounces of yarn, use these amounts:

+ 1 tablespoon of alum plus
+ 1 teaspoon of cream of tartar
+ $^1/_2$ teaspoon of tin
+ $1^1/_2$ teaspoons of copper
+ $1^1/_2$ teaspoons of iron
+ $^3/_4$ teaspoon of chrome

3. For greater accuracy, measure both the fiber and the mordants by weight in grams, and follow a percentage system. For 100 grams of wool, use:

+ 14 grams (14 percent of 100) alum plus 5 grams (4 percent) cream of tartar
+ 2 grams (2 percent) tin
+ 8 grams (8 percent) copper
+ 6 grams (6 percent) iron
+ 4 grams (4 percent) chrome

(available from pharmacists or mail-order suppliers) in 4 gallons of water.

Put the dry or wet yarn in the alum solution and let it soak at room temperature for 12 to 24 hours. You don't need to simmer the yarn, so you may soak it in a plastic container. Rinse the yarn in plain water at room temperature, then put it in the tannic acid solution, and let it soak at room temperature for 12 to 24 hours longer. Rinse again and put the yarn back into the alum solution and let it soak for 12 to 24 hours. Then rinse the yarn and proceed with dyeing or dry and store it for future use. You can reuse the same solutions for another batch of yarn without adding any more alum or tannic acid.

Reusing and disposing of mordants

Another reason for doing all my mordanting in advance is so that I can reuse the same pot of mordant solution for successive batches of yarn. I've learned that the first batch of yarn can absorb only a fraction of the dissolved mordant. To reuse a leftover solution, add mordant at one-third the original rate for the second and subsequent batches. For example, when mordanting with copper, use $1^{1}/_{2}$ teaspoons for the first 4-ounce batch of yarn, then reuse the same solution, adding only $^{1}/_{2}$ teaspoon more copper for each consecutive 4-ounce batch of yarn. This system uses much less of the mordant chemicals than if you prepared fresh chemicals for each batch, so it saves money and reduces waste but still gives good results.

When I've finished mordanting all the yarn I want with one mordant, I dispose of the solution. I pour cooled aluminum and iron solutions around hollies, mountain laurels, hydrangeas, blueberries, and other plants that prefer acid soil. The same chemicals that are used for mordanting are recommended as soil conditioners for these plants—at much higher dosages than I ever apply. I pour tin and copper solutions on the gravel driveway, where they serve no good but do no harm. It isn't safe to discard chrome at home, so I store chrome solution in a sealed, labeled plastic jug and save it until my local landfill schedules a hazardous waste collection day.

GATHERING AND STORING DYE PLANTS

The individual entries in this book tell you what part(s) of each plant to pick for dyeing. As noted, different parts of a plant sometimes give different colors and you should keep them separate; in other cases it doesn't matter, and you can put leaves, stems, and flowers in the dyepot together.

Yellow bedstraw and madder are harvested all at once every few years by digging the roots when the plants are dormant, but for all the other plants discussed in this book, only the aboveground parts are used, and they are harvested during the growing season. In most cases, you can pick from the same plant repeatedly, gathering flowers every few days or leaves every few weeks. By midfall, or whenever you get tired of picking a little at a time, you can cut off whole plant tops and be done with them.

Dyeing is a seasonal activity for me. I like to dye outdoors when the weather is nice, and do almost all my dyeing with plants fresh-picked from the garden. By midfall, when the air is getting cold and the garden is getting bare, I'm ready to put away my dye equipment and come back inside for a winter of spinning and knitting or weaving. If you want to prolong the season, though, you can preserve certain dye plants, as noted in the individual descriptions. To store flowers such as dahlias or cosmos, pack them into plastic bags and put them in the freezer. They'll keep for several months, perhaps as long as a year. Saving flowers in the freezer means that you can do one big batch of dyeing at the end of the season instead of many little batches from week to week. Using frozen dye flowers is as convenient as cooking frozen vegetables: just drop them into a pot of boiling water.

To store bulky whole plant tops such as those of tansy or marigold, hang them in a dark dry place with good air circulation, spacing the bundled stems far enough apart that they don't touch, or spread them in a single layer on window screens supported so that air can flow underneath as well as over the plants. I've read that dried dye plants can be stored for years, but I've never kept any past the next year's spring cleaning. To use dry dye plants, crumble them into a pot, cover with warm water, and soak them for a few hours or overnight before heating the pot.

Making a dyebath

To make a dye, you first have to extract the pigment from the plant and dissolve it in water. This process, called making a dyebath, is like brewing a pot of tea. Put the plant parts in a dyepot, chopping any big stalks if necessary to fit them in, then add enough water to cover the plants and put the lid on the pot. Heat the water to boiling or simmering, as indicated in the individual plant entries, and maintain that temperature for the recommended time—usually about one hour. It never hurts and often helps to let the plant material soak in the cooling dyebath for several hours or overnight. This extra soaking time helps extract more of the pigment from the plant, allowing you to dye more yarn or make darker colors.

It's possible to simmer yarn and plant material together in the dyepot, a technique called simultaneous dyeing. That saves fuel—you only have to heat the pot once—but you're liable to end up with flecks of debris in your yarn. I'd rather have unblemished yarn, so I always filter the dyebath by pouring it through a wire strainer once or twice before I proceed with the dyeing.

Sometimes you can strain off the dyebath, add fresh water, and reuse the same plant material to make one or two more dyebaths. There is a limit, though, to the amount of pigment that you can get from any plant. Some plants yield much more color than others. On average, I use about 4 ounces of fresh plant material to dye 1 ounce of yarn, but sometimes I use as little as 1 ounce or as much as 8 ounces of plant material. These amounts are more than some dyers use, but I like rich, saturated colors. If you like pastel colors, you can use a lower ratio of plant material to yarn. It's a good habit to weigh the plant material before you make a dyebath so that you can predict how much yarn it will dye.

Dyeing yarn

While you're preparing the dyebath, weigh out a suitable amount of dry, premordanted yarn and put it in a pan of warm water to soak. (You may mix different kinds of yarn or yarn premordanted with different mordants in the same dyepot.) Soaking the yarn for an hour or so prepares it to absorb the dye more evenly than it would if you immersed it in the dyebath when dry. When it seems good and wet, add it to the strained dyebath. It should sink right in, not float on the surface, and there should be enough liquid in the dyepot to cover the yarn completely; if there isn't, add some hot water to the pot.

Slowly heat the pot to simmering or boiling, as noted for each plant, and maintain that temperature for the recommended time. Sometimes it takes only 10 or 15 minutes for the yarn to absorb a pretty color. In other cases, it takes an hour or more of simmering, followed by a day or more of soaking. In general, the longer you simmer and soak the yarn, the darker the color becomes. While the yarn is simmering and soaking, gently prod it with a rod or spoon to push all parts down into the dyebath, but don't stir it in circles—that tangles the yarn and can cause wool fibers to felt together.

To check the color, lift a skein out of the dyebath, let it drain briefly, and squeeze out the extra liquid (wear a thick rubber glove to protect your hand from the heat and the dye). The color is always darker when the yarn is wet than after it dries, but this gives you an idea of what to expect.

When it seems ready, remove the yarn from the dyebath and squeeze all the extra liquid back into the pot. Wash the yarn in warm water with some liquid dishwashing detergent and keep rinsing it until the water runs clear. Put the yarn in your washing machine and spin out the extra water, then hang the yarn in a warm, shady place to dry.

Depending on how much plant material you used and how much yarn you put in at first, you can often reuse a dyebath to dye successive batches of yarn, resulting in a series of paler or different colors. This is called exhausting the dyebath or using an exhaust bath. When the colors become too weak or dull and aren't pretty anymore, you can dispose of a dyebath by pouring it on the ground.

Dyebath additives and afterdips

Directions for some of the plants discussed in this book suggest variations on the basic dye procedure. Some pigments are sensitive to pH—the acidity or alkalinity of a dyebath—and turn different colors in responses to changes in pH. I sometimes add a little vinegar to make the dyebath more acidic or a little baking soda or ammonia to make it more alkaline. These substances aren't mordants and don't improve the permanence of a dye, but they sometimes increase the range of colors that may be obtained from a particular plant. Use only as much of an additive as required to produce a color change. An excess of baking soda or ammonia damages protein fibers; the yarn will collapse into shreds. Vinegar doesn't harm protein fibers, but it can weaken cellulose fibers.

Another way to change the pH is to fill separate pots with hot water and add 1/4 cup of vinegar to one pot and 1/4 cup of household ammonia to the other. Take a hot skein out of the dyebath and soak it briefly in one pot or the other. If the pigment is sensitive to pH, even a brief soaking will produce a color change. Often pH-induced color changes are stable to subsequent washings, but sometimes they are not, and when you wash the yarn later, the pigment may shift back to a color determined by the pH of your water supply as well as that of the soap or detergent you use.

Weak solutions of iron, copper, and tin mordants are sometimes used as dyebath additives or afterdips, usually to darken or intensify the color of yarn that has been premordanted with alum. I do this occasionally, measuring one-quarter the normal amount of iron, copper, or tin for the weight of the yarn. After dyeing the yarn as usual, I add the extra mordant, dissolved in a small amount of water, to the dyebath and simmer the yarn until its color changes, or put the extra mordant solution in a different pot and simmer or soak the yarn there, to avoid contaminating the dyebath.

DYEING WITH FRESH INDIGO, JAPANESE INDIGO, OR WOAD LEAVES

Different as they are in other ways, indigo, Japanese indigo, and woad all produce the blue pigment called indigo. In every case, the traditional methods for using the indigo from these plants have involved processing large quantities of the leaves to extract and concentrate the pigment into solid lumps of blue stuff which could be stored indefinitely. For dyeing, the blue lumps had to be ground into a fine powder, dissolved in a vat of stale urine, and fermented for several weeks. All in all, it was a tricky, slow, and smelly process.

My modern method of using indigo is easy, fast, and virtually odorless. It's a practical way to use the leaves from a small patch or row of plants and to dye enough yarn for a hat, a scarf, or pair of mittens. I start with the fresh leaves, extract the dye, and use it right away. From start to finish, the process takes only about four hours.

Dyeing with fresh indigo is just as easy as using other dye plants, but the process is quite different. You don't boil the leaves or simmer the dyebath, and you don't have to

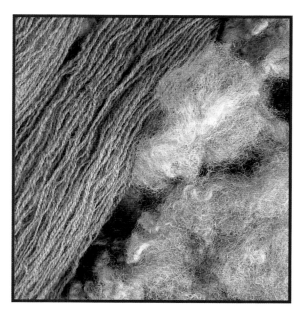

mordant the yarn. You do need one special ingredient called a reducing agent. My favorite reducing agent is Spectralite, an inexpensive white powder sold in small packets by dye suppliers. Order an ounce at a time and get a new supply every year or two, as Spectralite has a short shelflife.

For this recipe, use 8 ounces of indigo or Japanese indigo leaves or 32 ounces of woad leaves. (Because the pigment in woad is less concentrated, it takes more leaves to get as much color.) This will be enough to dye 2 to 4 ounces of fiber, depending on what fiber you dye and how dark a blue you want.

1. Pick fresh leaves and immediately put them into a clean, heat-resistant container. This doesn't have to be a metal dyepot—it can be a large glass jar or a heavy-duty plastic tub or pail. You don't have to shred or grind the leaves; just put them in whole.

2. There are two ways to extract the pigment from the leaves. In the case of woad, pour almost-boiling water over the leaves to scald them, using just enough water to cover the leaves. Cover the container and let it stand about one hour.

When using indigo or Japanese indigo leaves, add just enough hot tap water to cover the leaves, cover the container, set it into a larger pan of water (like using a double boiler), and put the two containers on the stove. Over low heat and using a thermometer to monitor the temperature, heat the water in the pot to 160°F over a period of about two hours.

3. The remaining steps are the same for all three plants. Strain off the dark, warm fluid into another pot. Wearing rubber gloves, squeeze the fluid out of the leaves and add it to the strained fluid. Discard indigo leaves now. You may boil Japanese indigo or woad to make completely different colors.

4. The dark fluid contains a precursor of indigo called indoxyl. Add one tablespoon of baking soda or ammonia to the fluid to make it alkaline, then pour the fluid back and forth from one container to another. As the indoxyl reacts with oxygen in the air, it will change into indigo, and the solution will turn to a dark blue-green or blue-brown. Keep pouring it back and forth for a few minutes.

5. The indigo isn't ready to use at this point. To prepare it for dyeing, it must be converted from the blue form into a yellowish form. That's what the reducing agent does. Dissolve 1 tablespoon of fresh Spectralite, or 2 tablespoons of an older package that might be getting stale, in a jar of warm water. Pour it into the dark dyebath and stir briefly. Cover the container and set it in a larger container of water just hot enough to keep the dyebath at a temperature of 100° to 120°F. Don't overheat it.

6. Meanwhile, put the yarn in hot water to soak. While the yarn does not have to be mordanted, it must be good and clean. You may dye the yarn all at once or divide it into two or more batches and dye them separately to get different shades of blue.

7. After an hour or so, when the dyebath has turned yellow, add the wet yarn, carefully lowering it down below the surface. Leave it to soak for 20 minutes or more, then gently lift it out of the dyebath. Like a miracle, the yarn will turn from yellow to blue as

it reacts with oxygen in the air. Let the yarn dry in the air for as long as it soaked in the bath. One dipping and airing is usually enough to give rich colors on wool yarn, but to intensify the colors on cotton or silk yarn, repeat the soaking and airing two or more times. After the final airing, wash and rinse the yarn.

8. You can put two, three, or more successive batches of yarn into the same indigo dyebath, getting lighter colors each time, until the pigment is all used up and the yarn no longer turns blue. Then discard the dyebath (it's safe to pour it down the drain) and scrub any stains out of the pot.

Troubleshooting

In ten years of growing and dyeing with fresh indigo, Japanese indigo, and woad, I've only had a few disappointments, but things *can* go wrong. If you don't get a good blue, here are some possible explanations:

✦ You picked leaves too early or too late in the season.

✦ You let the picked leaves sit around before heating them in water.

✦ You didn't heat the water enough, or you heated it too fast, or the water overheated and the leaves got boiled.

✦ You forget to add the baking soda or ammonia, or you added too much.

✦ The Spectralite was stale, and/or you didn't use enough.

✦ You tried to dye too much yarn for the amount of leaves that you had.

✦ You abandoned the dyebath for a day or longer. If not used promptly, it can go bad. I've tried several methods of storing the leaves or dyebaths such as freezing or sealing in airtight jars, but haven't found any system that works reliably or well. For best results, go straight through the dye process without delay.

Five

COLORS AND COLORS

*D*espite its long history and wide popularity, dyeing with plants still has many unanswered questions. Most of these have to do with color. What color(s) can you get from a particular plant? Why do different dyers get different results from the same plant? Is it possible to achieve consistent, predictable results? Can you follow a recipe to obtain the color you want, or is dyeing a matter of serendipity and luck? A group of dyers can discuss these questions into the night and never reach agreement. We all have different experiences, attitudes, and answers.

Reliability and predictability matter to people who are custom-dyeing yarn to sell, to use in historic reproductions, or to create particular textiles. In these situations, a dyer may have to produce a specific color and to get it just right, every time. It's definitely possible to do this with dyes from plants. Professional dyers of old took great pride in their ability to achieve consistent results, and some dyers do that today. How do they do it? They rely on a limited group of familiar dye plants, usually purchasing most of their supplies, and they don't experiment with unknown plants. They often specialize in a particular form—unspun fiber, yarn, or fabric—of a particular fiber—wool, cotton, silk, etc.—and develop habits and techniques for working with that material. They use laboratory-quality equipment to carefully weigh and measure the dyestuff, fiber, and mordant for each dye batch. They monitor the temperature of the dyebath and watch the clock. They keep detailed notes, save samples, and study their results. You can do this, too. It's not difficult; it's just a matter of working deliberately to achieve a goal.

Most amateur dyers don't work that way. I usually don't, myself. I used to strive for consistency, but I got bored with that. The truth is, I hardly ever need or want to produce or reproduce an exact shade. Coming close is almost always good enough for me. I don't mind a surprise now and then, and I welcome any color if it's bright and permanent. That's the perspective I bring to this book. I can't promise that your yarn will turn out exactly like my yarn, just as your garden won't look exactly like my garden, but if you follow my general directions, I'm sure that your colors will be pretty and you'll have a lot of fun.

Why do results differ from one time to the next? Why do different dyers get different colors from the same kind of plants? Many dyers dismiss these questions with a simple answer: it's all in the soil. From my own observations—speaking as both a gardener and a dyer—the soil a plant was grown in has very little to do with the colors that can be obtained from a dyebath made from that plant. Soil is just one factor out of many, and not a major one. Others include

- ✦ moisture and temperature during the growing season
- ✦ the plant's stage of growth or maturity
- ✦ what part of the plant was gathered
- ✦ whether it was used promptly or stored
- ✦ how long the dyebath was simmered and/or soaked
- ✦ the mineral content and pH of the water in the dyebath
- ✦ how much of which mordant was used, and when and how it was applied to the yarn
- ✦ the kind of fiber being dyed
- ✦ the ratio of dye plant to fiber

◆ how long the yarn was simmered and at what temperature

◆ whether the yarn was left to soak in the dyebath

It's daunting to think about all these variables and tedious to keep track of them in your notebook, but any one of them can make a little difference, or sometimes a big difference, between the color I get and the color you get from the same kind of plant, or the color you get in 1995 and the color you get in 1996. Now instead of worrying about how to match a color, let's turn the question around and think about how to get as many colors as possible—the more, the merrier—from your dye garden. For me, this is the difference between work and play. To multiply your colors, try these tips:

◆ Pick the right part of the plant at the recommended season or stage of growth.

◆ Make strong dyebaths, using plenty of plant material, and dye only a modest quantity of yarn at a time. Divide the yarn into a few small batches and dye them one at a time. You'll get more variety and richer colors this way.

◆ Put several small skeins into a strong dyepot at once but take them out one at a time after simmering for 15, 30, 45, or 60 minutes. Let some skeins soak in the cooling dyebath, and remove them after 1, 4, 12, or 24 hours.

◆ Dye different kinds of yarn spun from different fibers. Even different brands of white wool yarn absorb slightly different colors.

◆ Use different mordants. This often yields different colors from the same pot. Use pots made from different metals—steel, aluminum, copper, iron—if you have them.

◆ Use vinegar or ammonia afterdips to change the color of pH-sensitive dyes.

◆ Try another source of water—rainwater instead of tap water, distilled water instead of well water—to see if that affects your colors.

◆ Create new colors by moving yarn from one dyepot to another. This procedure, called top-dyeing, is a traditional way to create green, by following yellow with blue. Start by dyeing the yarn bright yellow with weld, goldenrod, broom sedge, or another yellow dye, then give the yellow yarn a brief dip (sometimes as little as 5 minutes will do) in an indigo dyepot. I often use top-dyeing to enhance or alter colors that were originally dull or common.

◆ Combine two plants in the same dyebath. This works best if both plants give clear strong colors, as coreopsis and marigolds do, for example. If either plant gives dull colors, or if you combine two weak leftover dyebaths, the result may look muddy.

S ix

A PORTFOLIO OF DYE GARDEN PLANTS

*T*he following entries highlight plants that you can grow to use for dyeing. Each entry includes a photograph of the plant, to show you what it looks like; a photo of yarn samples dyed with that plant, to give you an idea of the dye colors it can produce; and guidelines for how to grow the plant and how to use it for dyeing.

Each entry begins with the plant's **common** and **Latin** names. It may be listed under one name, the other, or both when you look for it in seed and plant catalogs. Most of the entries feature an individual species, but a few entries combine two or more species that look and grow about the same and give similar dye results.

Annual means that the plant germinates, grows, flowers, bears seeds, and dies in a single year's growing season. **Biennial** means the plant starts growing one year, survives over the winter, then flowers, sets seeds, and dies the second year. **Perennial** means the plant comes back year after year, unless something happens to kill it. The **zone** number is a code gardeners use to describe a plant's ability to endure cold temperatures, or its cold hardiness. The country is mapped into different hardiness zones, ranging from Zone 3 across the upper Great Plains to Zone 10 in southern Florida and coastal California, where it hardly ever gets down to freezing. If you don't know what zone you live in, ask the staff at a local nursery.

Height tells how tall the plant is likely to grow. This is an average—your plants might be shorter or taller. **Spacing** tells how much space the plant needs. Some plants spread to fill several square feet. Other plants can be crowded closer together with two or more plants per square foot. **Yield** gives a number for how many plants you need in order to dye four ounces of wool to a medium or dark color. Again, this is an average based on my experience. You might choose to use fewer or more plants.

The **plant photograph** shows the plant in midsummer, and features the part(s) of the plant that are used for dyeing (except for roots, which aren't shown). The **description** supplements the photograph to give you more information about what the plant looks like and how it grows. **Related species** describes other plants that are sometimes compared to, substituted for, or confused with the main entry.

How to grow tells how much sun, what kind of soil, and how much watering the plant needs, as well as how to get it started and how to care for it throughout the growing season.

The **dyed yarn samples** show some of the colors you can get from the plant, to help you decide whether or not you want to grow it. These are some of the colors you *can* get, not necessarily the exact colors you *will* get, because every dye lot is unique, just as every garden is unique. The **dyeing directions** tell you how to get colors similar to those shown, and sometimes give suggestions for how to further increase the range of colors. The samples are briefly labelled to identify fiber type, which premordant was used, any additive or afterdip that was used, and unusually short or long simmering and soaking. These variations are all discussed on pages 32–44.

Yellow bedstraw
(Galium verum)

Perennial. Zone 4.
Height: 2 to 3 feet.
Spacing: 1 plant spreads to fill 4 or more square feet.
Yield: The roots from 4 plants can dye 4 ounces of wool.

Description

Yellow bedstraw is a European wildflower with many herbal attributes: it's been used for stuffing mattresses, curdling milk to make cheese, treating minor wounds, soaking tired feet, and tinting hair. The tops give unremarkable yellow dyes, but the roots contain the same pigment as madder (see page 52) and give good red dyes. In this country, yellow bedstraw is often planted in herb gardens, and it has naturalized along roadsides in the northeastern states. It spreads to make a patch of many slender stems ringed with whorls of needlelike leaves and topped with foamy masses of bright gold flowers, starting in early summer. After bloom, the tall stalks look like unmown grass; if you shear them off, new low growth carpets the ground like a patch of prickly moss. Although I can't detect any fragrance in this plant, many references say the flowers are scented like honey and the dry foliage like vanilla.

Related species

There are hundreds of look-alike species in the genus *Galium* and the closely related genus *Asperula*. Only a few are cultivated, but others grow wild across North America. Some, but not all, produce the red dye in their roots. I've never gotten any dye from sweet woodruff (*G. odoratum*), cleavers (*G. aparine*), or northern bedstraw (*G. boreale*) but have had success with wild madder (*G. mollugo*) and dyer's woodruff (*G. tinctorium* or *Asperula tinctoria*).

How to Grow

Full sun. Yellow bedstraw grows best in moist but well-drained sandy soil. It spreads fast by underground runners and can overtake a garden, so make a special place for it by building a small edged bed or half-burying a bottomless container. If you fill the bed with a 50/50 mixture of coarse sand and garden soil, you'll be able to harvest the roots easily and efficiently without disturbing any adjacent plants. Yellow bedstraw grows readily from seeds, but seeds are rarely listed in catalogs. Buy one or more plants of yellow bedstraw from an herb nursery, and you can propagate it by division in spring or fall.

Dyeing with yellow bedstraw

The tops of yellow bedstraw, gathered in full bloom and simmered, give various shades of dull gold and yellow, but it's so easy to get these colors from other plants that I'd rather leave the bedstraw flowers in the garden and enjoy them there.

The roots, however, give a wide range of red, brick, and coral colors, depending on mordant and concentration. Dig the gnarly, woody roots in late fall, after the tops have died down, from plants that have been established for at least two years. Use the roots fresh or dry them for later use. When you're ready to use them, chop them with pruning shears into inch-long sections, cover with water, simmer for one hour, soak overnight, and strain off the dark red dyebath. Add fresh water to the roots, and repeat the simmering and soaking until no more color is released. You may pool the dyebaths together or use each one as you prepare it.

To dye, add mordanted yarn, simmer for one hour, let the yarn cool in the dyebath, and rinse. I've used this dye only on wool, but like madder, it should work on silk and cotton, too.

FLOWERING SHOOTS IN FULL BLOOM

Alum on silk

Alum on wool

Tin on wool

FRESH ROOTS DUG IN FALL

Alum on wool, exhaust

Alum on wool

Chrome on wool

Madder
(Rubia tinctorum)

Perennial. Zone 4.
Height: 2 feet.
Spacing: 1 plant spreads to fill 4 or more square feet.
Yield: The roots from 2 plants can dye 4 ounces of wool.

Description

Madder is a dull, even weedy plant with a secret. Its top growth is scratchy and sprawling, with whorls of plain green leaves and clusters of pale little flowers, but underground its tangle of pencil-thick woody roots are bright red inside. These roots have been used for centuries to make the red dye for calico-print cottons, Persian carpets, paisley shawls, and other textiles. Madder is native to the dry climates of south-central Asia, but it adapts well to diverse climates throughout the United States.

Related species

There are several other species of madder, but they are rarely cultivated. Roots are gathered from wild plants in parts of Asia where natural dyes are still being used.

How to grow

Full sun. Madder grows in any garden soil, but produces the best roots with the most dye if planted in deep, fertile, well-drained soil amended with plenty of ground limestone if your soil is on the acid side. It's worth preparing a special raised bed for madder to confine the roots and make it easy to find and harvest them. You can buy one plant from an herb nursery to get started and propagate it by division the next spring, or raise several plants at a time by starting with seeds. Sow the seeds indoors 8 weeks before the last frost and transplant into the bed when they are a few inches tall. Once established, madder keeps going indefinitely and requires virtually no care.

Dyeing with madder

At least two years after planting the bed, dig the madder roots in fall or spring, when the plant is dormant. Wash off the soil, cut the roots into short pieces, and use them immediately or dry them for later use.

There are dozens of recipes for dyeing with madder. The challenge is to get a clear red. Often, dyers get shades of coral, salmon, dark orange, or brick red, all of which you can get more easily and quickly (both in terms of growing the plants and dyeing the yarn) from dyer's coreopsis or yellow cosmos.

Grind the dry chopped madder roots in a blender and put them in a pot with just enough water to cover. Add a tablespoon of ground limestone or chalk dust (to enhance the red pigment). Lay a sheet of plastic wrap on the surface to prevent mold and let the madder soak for a month or more at room temperature. Then heat it to about 180°F, simmer for one hour, and strain off the dyebath into another dyepot. Add more water and repeat simmering and straining several times. When the second dyepot is full, strain the liquid again by pouring it through a fine fabric to catch any small particles that would otherwise stick to the yarn.

To dye, add mordanted yarn, heat to about 180°F, simmer for one hour, let the yarn soak in the dyebath for at least one day, then rinse it. You can reuse the same dyebath many times for a series of gradually paler and different colors ranging from red and brick red to orange, salmon, and coral. Using different mordants gives slightly different colors, but the difference between red and orange depends more on the quality of the madder and the strength of the dyebath than on the mordant.

DRIED ROOTS

Alum on cotton

Alum on wool

Alum on silk

Alum on wool

Alum on wool

Tin on wool

Chrome on wool

Yellow cosmos
(Cosmos sulphureus)

Annual. All zones.
Height: 1 to 3 feet.
Spacing: 2 plants per square foot.
Yield: The flowers from 12 plants can dye 4 ounces of wool.

Description

Yellow cosmos is a cheery annual that thrives in hot, dry weather. It blooms all summer, bearing bright yellow, orange, or red blossoms 1 to 2 inches wide on stiff stalks above a bushy mound of lacy dark green leaves. Butterflies visit the flowers for nectar and goldfinches flock to eat the ripe seeds. 'Diablo', 'Bright Lights', and 'Sunny Red' are popular cultivars listed in most seed catalogs.

Related species

Garden cosmos (*Cosmos bipinnatus*) grows 4 to 6 feet tall and has white, pink, rose, or crimson flowers up to 4 inches wide. It's a lovely annual for the flower garden but not a good dye plant.

How to grow

Full sun. Yellow cosmos thrives in average garden soil but also tolerates infertile or unimproved soil. Give it a weekly soaking during long dry spells. Sow purchased seeds indoors 6 weeks before the last frost, or directly in the garden after frost. Pick faded flowers twice weekly to use for dyeing and to prolong the flowering season. Yellow cosmos may self-sow if you let some seed heads mature at the end of the season, but a more reliable course is to harvest and store some seeds or buy new ones and plant them yourself the next spring.

Dyeing with yellow cosmos

Pick the blossoms every few days to keep the plants blooming all summer. Use them fresh or dry or freeze them for later use. There's little advantage in separating the flowers by color; they all yield similar dyes. Cover them with water, simmer for one hour, and strain off the bright red-orange dyebath. If the flowers aren't completely bleached out, add more water and simmer them again.

To dye, add mordanted yarn and simmer 15 to 60 minutes. Let the yarn soak overnight in the dyebath to obtain darker colors. Yellow cosmos gives various shades of orange on cotton, silk and wool. Mordanting with alum gives pale, medium, or golden oranges. Using tin makes a shocking "Koolaid" orange. Chrome, copper and iron give dark burnt orange or rusty brown. Adding a teaspoon of ammonia or baking soda to the dyebath shifts it to red and gives a brick red on alum-mordanted wool. Be careful not to add too much ammonia or baking soda and don't use either in combination with a tin mordant, or you may damage the wool. Although it's safer to dip the dyed skeins in an ammonia afterdip, that just gives a dark orange, not a brick red. In any case, rinse the yarn well after dyeing.

FRESH AND FROZEN FLOWER HEADS, MIXED COLORS

Alum on cotton

Alum on silk

Alum on wool

Alum on wool, ammonia dip

Tin on wool

Tin on wool

Chrome on wool

Dyer's coreopsis
(*Coreopsis tinctoria*, sometimes listed as *Calliopsis tinctoria*)

Annual. All zones.
Height: 1 to 2 feet.
Spacing: 2 plants per square foot.
Yield: The tops of 6 to 8 plants can dye 4 ounces of wool.

Description

Dyer's coreopsis, a prairie wildflower native to the Great Plains, is one of the easiest and most satisfactory plants for a dyer to grow. It bears hundreds of gold, maroon, red, or bicolor blossoms, each the size of a penny, over a span of 6 weeks or more in early to midsummer. Normally, dyer's coreopis grows tall and narrow as a clump of prairie grass, with slender stalks that wave in the wind, but a dwarf form that comes true from seed makes shorter, bushier plants. I've noticed, too, that when seeds germinate in the fall and overwinter as seedlings (instead of sprouting in the spring, as usual), they develop into compact, spherical plants instead of airy, upright plants.

Related species

Other species of coreopsis, including *Coreopsis lanceolata* and *C. grandiflora* (see page 58), are also good dye plants.

How to grow

Full sun. Grow dyer's coreopsis in average garden soil and water during dry spells to get the most flowers over the longest season. In infertile soil and dry weather, the plants go to seed sooner and may die out by midsummer. You can buy seeds from most mail-order seed catalogs. Sow them in the garden after danger of frost is past and thin the seedlings to stand 6 inches apart. Picking off individual flower heads as they fade or cutting the plants back halfway when the first flowers to open have gone to seed helps prolong the flowering season, but an easier way to have flowers in late summer and fall is to sow a second batch of seeds 6 weeks after the first. If you let some of the flowers go to seed, dyer's coreopsis may self-sow. Look for volunteer seedlings in late fall or early spring and weed around them or transplant them wherever you choose.

Dyeing with dyer's coreopsis

For years, I tediously picked individual flower heads of dyer's coreopsis, separating them by color because I thought the dark red or maroon ones must surely be more valuable than the yellow ones. Finally I got tired of that and tried chopping up whole plant tops—stems, leaves, different-colored flowers and seedheads—and got virtually the same range of colors in the dyebath. It's easy to uproot or cut back entire plants during or just after peak bloom; you can use them fresh or dry or freeze them for later use. Chop the plants into pieces so that you can push them down into the dyepot, cover with water, boil 30 minutes, and strain. There's a lot of pigment in these plants: you can reuse the same plant material to make two or three dyebaths.

To dye, add mordanted yarn, simmer for 15 to 60 minutes, cool, and rinse. For darker colors, let the dyed yarn soak overnight in the dyebath before rinsing. Dyer's coreopsis gives many shades of yellow, tan, gold, orange, rusty red, and brown, varying with dyebath concentration, simmering and soaking time, and mordant. Adding a teaspoon of baking soda or ammonia to the dyebath can produce madderlike reds, but be careful not to add too much, as wool is easily damaged by alkaline solutions. Using an ammonia afterdip is safer but doesn't give as good a red.

FRESH & FROZEN FLOWER HEADS, MIXED COLORS

Alum on cotton

Alum on silk

Alum on wool

Alum on wool

Copper on wool

Tin on wool

Tin on wool

Chrome on wool

WHOLE PLANTS AFTER PEAK BLOOMS

Alum on cotton

Alum on silk

Alum on wool

Copper on wool

Tin on wool

Chrome on wool

Coreopsis
(Cultivars of *Coreopsis grandiflora* and *C. lanceolata*)

Hardy perennial. Zone 5
Height: 1 to 2 feet
Spacing: 1 plant needs 2 to 3 square feet
Yield: The tops and flowers of 2 or 3 plants can dye 4 ounces of wool.

Description

These two very similar species are southeastern wildflowers that bloom for several weeks in early summer, with bright gold daisylike blossoms held on slender, branched stalks above a basal mound of dark green, deeply lobed leaves. The wild forms have tall, weak stalks that tend to flop over. Hybrid cultivars such as 'Early Sunrise', 'Sunburst', and 'Sunray' are more compact with stronger stems, and they bloom for a longer season, from early summer until fall.

Related species

The annual dyer's coreopsis (*Coreopsis tinctoria*, page 56) is one of the best-known dye plants. Other species can also be used, mostly yielding shades of gold. One of the prettiest selections is *C. verticillata* 'Moonbeam', a popular perennial that makes a dense clump of dark, feathery foliage topped with pale yellow blossoms for weeks in midsummer.

How to grow

Full or part sun. Coreopsis grows best in average garden soil but tolerates dry, infertile soil. Buy plants from a local nursery or raise your own from seeds. The seeds germinate readily and grow quickly, indoors or out, but seedlings usually don't bloom until the second year. Pick blossoms regularly to prolong the flowering period; when the stalks are bare, cut them off. Divide established plants every second or third year in spring or fall.

Dyeing with coreopsis

Gather whole plant tops or just the flower heads throughout the summer to use fresh. You may dry or freeze them for later use. Cover with water, boil for 30 minutes, and strain off the dark reddish brown dyebath. You can usually reuse the same batch of plant material to make a second dyebath that's almost as strong as the first.

To dye, add mordanted yarn, simmer for 15 to 60 minutes, cool, and rinse. A dye made from the flower heads alone gives yellows and golds. Using entire plant tops gives a wider range of darker shades—tan, gold, orange, rust, and brown—depending on mordant, dyebath concentration, and simmering time. An ammonia afterdip darkens and intensifies the colors. Coreopsis works best on wool and silk: colors are paler on cotton.

WHOLE PLANT TOPS IN FULL BLOOM

Alum on cotton

Alum on silk

Alum on wool

Copper on wool

Tin on wool

Chrome on wool

Dahlia
(*Dahlia* hybrids)

Tender perennial, grown as an annual. All zones.
Height: 1 to 5 feet, depending on cultivar.
Spacing: 1 plant needs 1 to 4 square feet, depending on cultivar.
Yield: The flowers from 4 to 8 plants can dye 4 ounces of wool.

Description

Dahlias are grown for their gorgeous blossoms, which come in all colors but blue and in many shapes and sizes—as small and round as a golf ball, as big and flat as a dinner plate, or any combination in between. All dahlia flowers give lovely colors in the dyepot. The plants are bushy with several sturdy stalks and dark green compound leaves. Compact forms make colorful bedding plants, and the taller, long-stalked cultivars provide excellent cut flowers.

Related species

There are wild dahlias in Mexico and Central America, but nearly all of the dahlias grown in gardens are hybrid forms. It seems incredible—can there really be so many kinds of dahlias?—but the International Register of Dahlia Names lists 20,000 cultivars.

How to grow

Full sun in most areas, afternoon shade where summers are hot. Dahlias need well-drained, fertile soil and regular watering. You can grow them from tubers or from seeds. For the biggest and fanciest flowers, buy tubers from a local or mail-order nursery. Plant them 4 inches deep and 1 to 3 feet apart after the last frost. For flowers that are less extraordinary but perfectly good for dyeing, buy a packet of dahlia seeds. Sow the seeds indoors in individual pots 6 weeks before the last frost, or directly in the garden when the soil is warm. The seedlings grow fast and bloom the first year. To save a favorite dahlia from year to year, dig the clump of tubers in the fall, shake off the soil, hang it upside down to dry, then store the whole clump in a paper bag in a cool, dark place. Separate the tubers carefully in spring and replant the ones with the most vigorous buds and shoots.

Dyeing with dahlias

Gather whole flower heads just as they pass their prime, picking them from the garden or the vase. Use them fresh or freeze them for later use. It isn't worth separating the flowers by color except to discard white flowers, which produce little color. Red, purple, pink, orange, and yellow dahlias all give similar dyes. Cover the flowers with water, boil 30 minutes, and strain. The flowers will look bleached, and the dyebath will be dark orange.

To dye, add mordanted yarn and simmer 30 to 60 minutes. Dahlias give all the shades of a sunset—yellow, gold, peach, orange and rusty orange—on wool, silk and cotton. Using different mordants gives different colors. An ammonia afterdip helps darken and intensify the colors.

FRESH AND FROZEN FLOWER HEADS, MIXED COLORS

Alum on cotton

Alum on silk

Alum on wool

Alum on wool

Alum on wool, ammonia dip

Copper on wool

Tin on wool

Chrome on wool

Marigold
(*Tagetes erecta, T. patula,* and hybrids)

Annual. All zones.
Height: 1 to 2 feet.
Spacing: 1 plant per square foot.
Yield: The flowers and leaves from 4 to 6 plants can dye 4 ounces of wool.

Description

Marigolds are familiar bedding plants in all parts of the United States because they are inexpensive and easy to grow and they bloom for months. The plants can be compact or upright, but they're always bushy and well branched with pungent, dark green fernlike foliage and plump, rounded flower heads 1 to 4 inches wide. The tall, or African types (*Tagetes erecta*) have bright yellow or orange blossoms, except for the so-called white marigold, which is actually cream-colored. The dwarf, or French marigolds (*T. patula*) have yellow, orange, rusty red, or bicolor blossoms.

Related species

Other marigolds can be used for dyeing, but they give fewer and paler colors than common marigolds do. Some of my favorites are 'Lemon Gem' marigold (*T. tenuifolia* 'Lemon Gem'), an annual with single, clear yellow flowers and fine-textured, lemon-scented foliage, and Mexican mint marigold (*T. lucida*), a tender (Zone 8) perennial with small gold flowers in early fall and anise-scented foliage that's used as a tarragon substitute and in herbal teas.

How to grow

Full sun. Marigolds thrive in any well-drained garden soil. They tolerate hot weather but need occasional watering during long dry spells. Buy transplants at any garden center in spring or grow your own plants from seeds. Sow the seeds indoors 6 to 8 weeks before the last frost or directly in the garden when the soil is warm. When the seedlings are a few inches tall, pinch off their tips to promote branching. Marigolds are generally pest-free, but Japanese beetles will eat the flowers. Wet soil, humid air, and excess rain can rot the roots, foliage, and flowers.

Dyeing with marigolds

Gather leaves, flower heads, or both anytime during the growing season to use fresh or dry or freeze for later use. Cover with water, simmer 30 minutes, and strain off the intensely colored dyebath. Marigolds have a strong smell, so work outdoors or with good ventilation.

To dye, add mordanted yarn, simmer 15 to 60 minutes, cool, and rinse. Marigolds make many good colors on wool, silk and cotton, varying with flower color, dyebath concentration, simmering time, and mordant. Changing the pH of the dyebath does not seem to affect the colors. Using the leaves alone gives soft and bright yellows and golds. The yellow and orange flowers give many shades of yellow, gold, and orange; the rusty red and bicolor flowers give these colors as well as tans and browns.

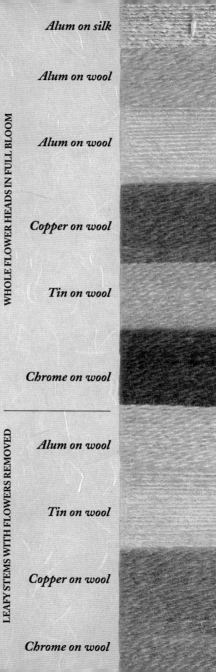

WHOLE FLOWER HEADS IN FULL BLOOM

Alum on silk

Alum on wool

Alum on wool

Copper on wool

Tin on wool

Chrome on wool

LEAFY STEMS WITH FLOWERS REMOVED

Alum on wool

Tin on wool

Copper on wool

Chrome on wool

Garland chrysanthemum
(Chrysanthemum coronarium)

Annual. All zones.
Height: 30 inches.
Spacing: 1 plant per square foot.
Yield: The flowers and leaves from 4 to 6 plants can dye 4 ounces of wool.

Description

This annual chrysanthemum bears little resemblance to the familiar "mums" that blossom in football season or the potted specimens sold by florists. It's a bushy plant that branches near the base into several sturdy, upright stems and blooms all summer with bright yellow flowers about 1 inch wide. This plant is grown as a vegetable in China and Japan and is sometimes listed in seed catalogs as edible chrysanthemum, chop suey green, or shungiku. The fragrant, bright green, finely divided leaves can be added to salads or stir-fries (young leaves are best; older leaves are likely to be tough and bitter).

Related species

They're all wonderful plants, but I've never gotten much of a dye from the garden or florist's chrysanthemum (*C. morifolium*), nor from marguerites (*C. frutescens*), shasta daisies (*C. superbum*), or any other species of chrysanthemum.

How to grow

Full sun. Garland chrysanthemum does best in fertile, well-drained soil with regular watering. It's carefree and easy to grow. You're unlikely to find plants locally, so mail-order a packet of seeds. Sow them indoors up to 8 weeks before the last frost, or directly in the garden about 2 weeks before the last frost. Here in New England, garland chrysanthemum thrives all summer and well into the fall, blooming nonstop from July through October. In hotter climates, plant two crops, one in early spring and a second in early fall.

Dyeing with garland chrysanthemum

Gather plant tops anytime during the growing season to use fresh or dry or freeze for later use. Cover with water, simmer for 30 to 60 minutes, and strain off the aromatic, dark gold dyebath.

To dye, add mordanted yarn, simmer 15 to 60 minutes, cool, and rinse. A dyebath made from the whole tops in bloom gives a range of tans, yellows, golds, oranges, olive greens, and browns on cotton, silk, and wool, varying with fiber and mordant. You can pick just the leaves or just the flowers and make separate dyebaths for even more variety. This is a rewarding dye plant that quickly makes a strong dyebath and gives a wide range of attractive colors.

WHOLE PLANT TOPS IN FULL BLOOM

Alum on cotton

Alum on silk

Alum on wool

Alum on wool

Chrome on wool

Goldenrod
(*Solidago* spp.)

Perennial. Most hardy to Zone 4.
Height: up to 5 feet.
Spacing: 1 plant needs 4 square feet.
Yield: The tops of 4 plants can dye 4 ounces of wool.

Description

Goldenrods are abundant wildflowers in most of the eastern United States, but they also make carefree, colorful garden plants. There are dozens of species and several cultivars to choose from. All spread to make a patch and send up many leafy stalks topped with fluffy clusters of tiny yellow or gold flowers. An individual plant blooms for 3 to 4 weeks, and different species flower in sequence from July to October. The blossoms attract many butterflies and make long-lasting cut flowers.

Related species

Perennial and native-plant nurseries offer many goldenrods. Some of the best—because they look showy and don't spread too fast—are *Solidago canadensis* 'Golden Baby', sweet goldenrod (*S. odora*), rough-leaved goldenrod (*S. rugosa*), seaside goldenrod (*S. sempervirens*), *S. sphacelata* 'Golden Fleece', and the European *S. virgaurea* 'Goldenmosa'. Any goldenrod can be used for dyeing.

How to grow

Full sun. Goldenrods thrive in any average soil with occasional watering. Some tolerate poor, dry soil. Seeds are rarely offered, so start with a plant from a nursery. If you want more later, you can divide the rhizomes in early spring. Except for minor insect pests and foliar diseases, goldenrods are generally trouble-free and long-lived.

Dyeing with goldenrods

Goldenrod works best if used fresh; dry material gives weaker, duller colors. You can harvest it twice for different results. In early summer, gather leafy shoots. You can thin the clump by cutting a few shoots to the ground, and cut off the top third of the remaining shoots; this will make them branch out. Later in the season, pick bunches of flowers anytime after they open and before they start to fade.

Put the leafy shoots or flowers in a dye-pot, cover with water, simmer 30 to 60 minutes, and strain. To dye, add mordanted fiber, simmer 10 to 60 minutes, cool, and rinse. The leafy shoots make a drab dyebath that gives shades of tan and brown. The flower heads produce a dark gold dyebath with a strong aroma (it smells like apple-sauce to me but makes some people sneeze) that gives bright yellows and golds. For the prettiest, clearest colors, remove the yarn after just 10 or 15 minutes. Longer simmering makes the colors darker but "dirtier". Using different mordants gives good color variation from a goldenrod dyebath, but changing dyebath pH has little effect.

TOPS OF FLOWERING STALKS IN FULL BLOOM

Alum on wool, 10-minute simmer

Alum on wool, 60-minute simmer

Tin on wool

Tin on wool

Chrome on wool

LEAFY SHOOTS JUST PRIOR TO BLOOM

Alum on cotton

Alum on wool

Copper on wool

Tansy
(Tanacetum vulgare)

Perennial. Zone 4.
Height: flower stalks up to 3 feet.
Spacing: 1 plant spreads to fill 4 or more square feet.
Yield: The tops of 4 plants can dye 4 ounces of wool.

Description

Tansy is an indomitable perennial that lingers in gardens long after their owners have moved on. Native to Europe, it has a long history as a medicinal herb and insect repellent. The bright green, finely divided foliage has a strong, penetrating aroma. The plant spreads by underground runners and sends up many leafy stems, each topped in summer with flat clusters of bright gold button-sized flower heads. If you want something special, get a plant of curly tansy (*Tanacetum vulgare* var. *crispum*), a selected variety with unusually dense, crisp-textured foliage.

Related species

There are other species of tansy, and recent reclassification has added costmary (formerly *Chrysantheum balsamita*) and feverfew (*C. parthenium*) to the genus *Tanacetum*, but none of these is a noteworthy dye plant.

How to grow

Full sun. Tansy grows in any well-drained soil and tolerates poor, dry sites. You can start it from seed (seedlings bloom the first year) or buy a plant at any herb nursery. It spreads fast by underground runners and can invade adjacent plantings. Give it plenty of space or bury a bottomless pot and plant the tansy inside to confine it, or dig and divide the plant annually, replanting part of it and discarding the rest.

Dyeing with tansy

Gather whole plant tops in summer or fall to use fresh or dry for later use. Cover with water, boil for one hour, and strain off the dyebath. Work outdoors or with good ventilation, for a tansy dyebath smells very strong.

To dye, add mordanted yarn, simmer 30 to 60 minutes, cool, and rinse. Tansy gives an attractive range of yellows, golds, and greens on cotton, silk, and wool. Try using different mordants—that makes a big difference. Dipping the dyed skeins in an ammonia solution can change the colors dramatically also. I've always used the whole tops, but separating the leaves from the flower heads to make two dyebaths might further expand the range of colors.

LEAFY SHOOTS AND FLOWER HEADS IN FULL BLOOM

Alum on cotton

Alum on silk

Alum on wool

Alum on wool, ammonia dip

Tin on wool

Copper on wool

Chrome on wool

Black-eyed Susan, coneflower
(*Rudbeckia fulgida* 'Goldsturm', *R.* spp.)

Hardy perennial. Zone 3.
Height: 2 to 3 feet.
Spacing: 1 plant needs 4 square feet.
Yield: The leaves and flowers of 12 plants can dye 4 ounces of wool.

Description

Black-eyed Susan is a popular perennial that's easy to grow, trouble-free, and blooms over a long season. In spring, it makes a low mound of large, oval, dark green rough-textured leaves. Dozens of stiff, erect, branched flower stalks rise from the center of the mound in midsummer, bearing daisylike blossoms 3 to 4 inches wide with bright golden rays around a thimble-sized dark brown disk. Bloom continues for 6 to 8 weeks or until hard frost, and the dry dark seed heads look interesting in fall and winter.

Related species

Other rudbeckias are also good dye plants that give similar colors. Orange coneflower (*Rudbeckia fulgida*), another species known as black-eyed Susan (*R. hirta*), sweet coneflower (*R. subtomentosa*), and thin-leaved coneflower (*R. triloba*) are common wildflowers in the central and eastern United States and are popular for meadow or prairie gardens.

The gloriosa daisy is a cultivated form of the annual *R. hirta* with gold, orange, red, mahogany, or multicolored blossoms up to 6 inches wide. It grows quickly from seeds and often self-sows.

How to grow

Full sun. Black-eyed Susan grows well in average garden soil if you water during dry spells to prevent wilting. It adapts well to heavy soil or damp sites. The cultivar 'Goldsturm' does come true from seeds, but it's faster to start with a plant from a nursery. It will make an impressive clump by the second or third year, and you can propagate it by division in spring or fall. This is a tough, reliable plant, hardy to cold and heat, and rarely bothered by pests or diseases.

Dyeing with black-eyed Susan

Gather leaves and/or flower heads (they give different colors, so keep them separate) anytime in summer and early fall. You may dry or freeze them for later use. It takes prolonged boiling and soaking to extract the pigment from black-eyed Susan. Cover with water, heat to a full boil—not just a simmer—and boil for one to two hours, then let the pot sit at room temperature for an additional day or two before straining off the dyebath. If the blossoms still look fresh and gold when you strain them out, you can put them back in and boil them longer. To dye, add mordanted yarn, simmer for at least one hour, then let it soak in the cooling dyebath for at least a day. It takes a strong dyebath to get saturated colors; weaker dyebaths give only shades of tan. The colors vary little with different mordants and don't react to vinegar or ammonia. The leaves and stems give shades of gold and dull orange, all with a very slight greenish cast. The flower heads give various shades of olive green and brownish green.

FLOWER HEADS IN FULL BLOOM

Alum on wool

Alum on silk

Alum on wool, exhaust

Copper on wool

Chrome on wool

LEAVES AND STEMS, NO FLOWERS

Alum on silk

Alum on wool

Chrome on wool

Dyer's chamomile, golden marguerite
(Anthemis tinctoria)

Perennial. Zone 3.
Height: 2 feet.
Spacing: 1 plant needs 2 square feet.
Yield: The leaves and flowers of 12 plants can dye 4 ounces of wool.

Description

Dyer's chamomile is a hardy perennial that bears masses of golden yellow daisies on slender stalks above a clump of fragrant gray-green, finely divided foliage. It blooms for several weeks in early to midsummer. Popular cultivars include 'Kelwayi', with bright yellow flowers, and 'Moonlight', with light yellow flowers.

Related species

Anthemis sancti-johannis is a similar species with orange flowers. Roman chamomile, formerly known as *A. nobilis*, is now classified as *Chamaemelum nobile*. Sometimes used as an herbal lawn or ground cover, it makes a dense flat mat of bright green, finely dissected leaves. Its tiny daisylike blossoms make an aromatic and soothing tea. These species can also be used for dyeing.

How to grow

Full sun or afternoon shade. Average or poor soil will do; if the soil is too rich, dyer's chamomile gets floppy and is subject to fungus infections. However, this plant wilts quickly in hot or dry weather and needs regular watering. It does best across the northern United States and along the Pacific Coast, where summers aren't too hot. You can buy plants from garden centers or perennial nurseries or grow your own from seeds. Sow seeds indoors 8 weeks before the last frost. The plants will bloom the first summer. To propagate named cultivars, divide the plants every other year in early spring.

Dyeing with dyer's chamomile

Gather leaves anytime during the growing season for fresh use. Pick flower heads individually as they fade, or wait until peak bloom is passed and cut entire flower stalks down to the ground. (Cutting off the spent stalks is a good idea whether or not you're going to use them for dyeing.) You may dry the material for later use. Cover the plant parts with water, boil 30 to 60 minutes, and strain off the dyebath. It will have a pleasant fragrance.

To dye, add mordanted yarn and simmer 30 to 60 minutes. The flower heads give typical yellows with alum on wool or silk and darker golds and oranges with tin or chrome. The leaves are more interesting because they give unusual—not just olive— shades of green.

FRESH FLOWER HEADS

Alum on silk

Alum on wool

LEAVES AND STEMS, NO FLOWERS

Tin on wool

Alum on wool

Copper on wool

Sunflower
(Helianthus annuus)

Annual. All zones.
Height: 4 to 6 feet or taller.
Spacing: 1 plant needs 2 to 4 square feet.
Yield: The flowers from 12 plants can dye 4 ounces of wool.

Description

Sunflowers aren't remarkable as dye plants, but they're cheerful and easy to grow and make a useful screen or backdrop for a large dye garden. In addition to the familiar type that makes a single giant golden blossom on a towering stalk, there are several strains that make bushy, much-branched plants with many smaller blossoms in shades of cream, yellow, orange, maroon, rust, mahogany and bicolor. Look in seed catalogs for 'Autumn Beauty', 'Color Fashion', 'Music Box', 'Velvet Queen', and other named cultivars. (Some of these new seed strains may be hybrids between *Helianthus annuus* and *H. debilis*, a similar species.)

Unfortunately, seeds for the sunflower most interesting to dyers are hard to find. That's the 'Hopi Black Dye' sunflower, a strain developed by the Hopi Indians of Arizona, who use its dark-hulled seeds (rather than the fresh flower heads) for dyeing.

Related species

Some of the perennial sunflowers are stunning plants, especially popular among native-plant gardeners. I haven't tried, but I expect that their flowers could be used for dyeing.

How to grow

Full sun. Sunflowers grow in any average garden soil. Sow the seeds directly in the garden, 1 inch deep, about the time of the average last frost date in spring. If you pinch off the tips when the seedlings are several inches tall, they'll grow more bushy and bear more flowers. Water deeply once a week during dry spells. Sunflowers attract bees and butterflies, and if you let some of the flowers go to seed, goldfinches and other birds will come to eat them.

Dyeing with sunflowers

Pick whole sunflower heads in full bloom and use them fresh. Cover with water, boil for an hour, leave to soak overnight, and strain off the dyebath.

To dye, add mordanted yarn, simmer for two hours, let the yarn soak in the dyebath for another day, then rinse. It takes prolonged simmering and soaking in a strong dyebath to get much color from sunflowers. On wool, the flowers give various shades of greenish gold, beige, and tan, depending on mordant. The dye is ineffective on cotton.

To use 'Hopi Black Dye' sunflower seeds, simmer them for 30 to 60 minutes and strain off the dark purple dyebath. The Hopi may use special techniques for dyeing wool and basketry materials as they get a range of very dark blues, blacks, and purples. With ordinary methods, I get mostly lilacs and grays.

WHOLE FLOWER HEADS IN FULL BLOOM

Alum on cotton

Alum on wool

Alum on wool

Alum on wool, copper dip

Tin on wool

Copper on wool

Yarrow
(*Achillea* hybrids)

Perennial. Zone 3.
Height: 2 feet.
Spacing: 1 plant needs 3 square feet.
Yield: The tops of 12 plants can dye 4 ounces of wool.

Description

Yarrow isn't a versatile dye plant, but it's certainly a reliable garden plant. The new hybrid yarrows, in particular, are popular among gardeners from coast to coast. They make a spreading mat or mound of fragrant, fernlike foliage that's evergreen in mild climates and blooms repeatedly from early summer until late fall. The tiny daisylike blossoms are clustered in dense, flat heads 2 to 6 inches wide atop stiff 2-foot stalks. They come in bright and pastel shades of yellow, pink, coral, rose, or red and make long-lasting cut flowers for fresh or dried arrangements. 'Debutante' and 'Summer Pastels' are mixed-color strains that you can grow from seeds. 'Paprika', 'Apple Blossom', 'Fanal', and other new hybrids from Germany are vegetatively propagated cultivars, so you can buy plants of specific colors.

Related species

Common yarrow (*Achillea millefolium*), a parent of the modern hybrids, grows wild in lawns, pastures, open woods, and roadsides across North America, Europe, and Asia. Long valued as a medicinal herb, it has pungent gray-green foliage and creamy white flowers. (A crimson-flowered form is also available.) Several other species and hybrids of yarrow are popular for perennial borders and rock gardens. Most give tan or gold dyes.

How to grow

Full or part sun. Yarrow grows best in average garden soil but tolerates any well-drained site. It's pest-free and very hardy to both cold and dry heat but gets foliar fungus diseases when the weather is hot and humid. Buy a plant from a nursery or sow seeds indoors 8 weeks before the last frost. (If sown early, seedlings flower the first summer.) Propagate purchased plants or outstanding seedlings by dividing them in spring or fall. Cut old stalks at the base when the flowers fade to encourage continuing bloom.

Dyeing with yarrow

Gather leaves and/or flower stalks anytime from spring to fall. Cover with water, simmer for one hour, and strain off the golden dyebath. Yarrow smells strong, so work outdoors or with good ventilation.

To dye, add mordanted yarn, simmer one hour, cool, and rinse. Yarrow gives mostly shades of yellow and gold on cotton, silk, and wool, whether you use leaves or flower heads. Using different mordants or ammonia has little effect on the color.

WHOLE PLANTS IN FULL BLOOM

Alum on cotton

Alum on silk

Alum on wool

Tin on wool

Copper on wool

Chrome on wool

Zinnia
(Zinnia elegans)

Annual. All zones.
Height: 1 to 3 feet.
Spacing: 1 plant per square foot.
Yield: The flowers from 16 to 24 plants can dye 4 ounces of wool.

Description

Zinnias are easy-to-grow annuals, popular as bedding plants and for long-lasting cut flowers. There are many strains; they produce blossoms 1 to 6 inches wide in shades of red, orange, pink, yellow, and white. They bloom for months, from early summer until frost. As dye plants, zinnias are much less desirable than dahlias, cosmos, or marigolds—it takes more zinnia blossoms to get fewer and duller colors than you get from the other flowers. But if space is unlimited, zinnias are a cheerful addition to any dye garden.

Related species

Mexican zinnia (*Zinnia haageana*) tolerates hot, dry weather better than common zinnias. It has bicolor flowers in shades of yellow, gold, red, mahogany, and maroon; 'Old Mexico' and 'Persian Carpet' are old but still-popular strains. The narrow-leaf zinnia (*Z. angustifolia*, formerly *Z. linearis*) makes a loose mound of thin stems with sparse narrow leaves but blooms throughout the hottest weather and bears scores of small orange or white blossoms. The desert zinnia or Rocky Mountain zinnia (*Z. grandiflora*) is a hardy perennial to Zone 5 that has bright yellow blossoms all summer and makes a tough ground cover for poor dry soil. The flowers of all these zinnias can be used for dyeing.

How to grow

Full sun. Zinnias grow best in good garden soil with regular watering. They tolerate heat but not drought. In humid weather, their foliage is subject to mildew, which disfigures and weakens the plants. Allow plenty of space between plants for good air circulation, and don't wet the foliage when watering.

Any garden center sells zinnia transplants in spring, but it's easy to grow your own plants from seeds. Sow the seeds indoors 6 weeks before the last frost or plant directly in the garden after the last frost, when the soil is warm. If you pick the flowers as soon as they fade, the plants will keep blooming all summer.

Dyeing with zinnias

Pick the flower heads before they fade and use them fresh. Don't bother separating red, orange, and pink flowers, but the darker flowers do yield more dye than yellow or white ones. Cover the flowers with water, simmer one hour, and strain them out of the bright-colored dyebath.

To dye, add mordanted fiber, simmer at least one hour, soak the yarn in the dyebath another day, then rinse. You may be surprised by the colors you get—mostly beiges, tans, and browns—all quite pretty but dull compared to the vivid dyebath and the sunny colors of the blossoms themselves.

FRESH FLOWER HEADS, BRIGHT RED

Alum on cotton

Alum on silk

Alum on wool

Alum on wool, ammonia dip

Copper on wool

Chrome on wool

Hardy hibiscus, rose mallow
(*Hibiscus* hybrids)

Perennial. Zone 5 or 6.
Height: 3 to 6 feet.
Spacing: 1 plant needs 4 square feet.
Yield: The flowers from 4 plants can dye 4 ounces of wool.

Description

The modern hardy hybrid hibiscus were developed from the native rose mallows that grow wild in sunny marshes along the eastern seacoast. What's remarkable is the size of their flowers, which measure up to 10 inches wide. Each flower lasts only one day, but new ones keep coming from midsummer until frost. The plants are bushy, with several stiff, unbranched stalks, and make a showy hedge, background, or centerpiece. Hybrids of 'Dixie Belle' (2 to 3 feet tall) and 'Southern Belle' (4 to 6 feet tall) are available as seeds or plants and have white, pink, or rosy red flowers. 'Lord Baltimore', sold only as plants, grows 5 feet tall with clear, bright red flowers. The red and rosy red flowers are by far the most valuable for dyeing.

Related species

The China rose, or tropical hibiscus (*Hibiscus rosa-sinensis*), grows well in a pot and blossoms nonstop on a sunny patio or windowsill. Rose-of-Sharon (*H. syriacus*) is a tough, hardy, old-fashioned shrub that flowers in the heat of summer. It's worth experimenting with the darkest flowers from these and other species of hibiscus.

How to grow

Full sun. Hardy hibiscus will grow in any good garden soil if watered during dry spells. It adapts well to heavy soil or damp sites. You can buy plants at most nurseries or raise them from seeds. The seedlings grow fast and bloom the first year if started indoors 8 weeks before the last frost. Other than being attractive to Japanese beetles, which can ravage both foliage and flowers, the plants are trouble-free and can live in the same spot for decades. Because they don't come up until late in the spring, plant some daffodils or tulips nearby to add color in the meantime.

Dyeing with hardy hibiscus

Pick the red or rosy red flowers every day or two. Pink hibiscus flowers just give golds and tans, and the white flowers aren't worth gathering. Discard the green calyx and save just the petals. You may store them in a plastic bag in the refrigerator for up to a week, but they don't dry or freeze well. Cover the flowers with water, simmer for 30 minutes, and strain. The dyebath will be thick and mucilaginous.

To dye, add mordanted yarn and simmer for one hour. For the darkest colors, let the yarn soak in the dyebath for a day or two after simmering. Dark hibiscus flowers give fascinating, impressive, but unpredictable colors on wool, silk, and cotton. The pigment is very sensitive to pH; adding vinegar or ammonia to the dyebath or dipping dyed skeins in either solution causes dramatic color shifts. Using different mordants gives different colors, too. Every time I use this plant, I get different colors—lilac, purple, mauve, green, gray, brown, black—but they're all interesting and attractive.

DARK ROSE-PINK FLOWERS

Alum on silk, pH7

Alum on wool, 3-day soak

Alum on cotton, vinegar dip

Alum on silk, vinegar dip

Alum on wool, vinegar dip

Alum on cotton, ammonia dip

Alum on wool, ammonia dip

No mordant on wool, 3-day soak

Tin on wool, 3-day soak

Chrome on wool, pH7

Hollyhock
(*Alcea rosea*, formerly *Althaea rosea*)

Usually biennial. Zone 5.
Height: 4 to 8 feet.
Spacing: 1 plant needs 4 square feet.
Yield: The flowers from 8 to 12 plants can dye 4 ounces of wool.

Description

Hollyhocks are colorful, easy-to-grow plants for old-fashioned or modern gardens. In good soil, a single plant will bear several towering flower stalks lined with dozens of flowers in colors ranging from white, yellow, pink, and rose to dark reddish black. Most nurseries sell the 'Chater's Doubles' or 'Powderpuff' types, which have double flowers packed with petals, but seeds for the old-fashioned single types are available by mail order.

Related species

Various species of *Malva, Malope* and *Lavatera* are popular garden plants with hollyhocklike flowers, but I haven't gotten exciting dye colors from any of them.

How to grow

Full sun. Hollyhocks form giant clumps and flower most profusely if planted in deep, rich, moist soil, but they also grow and bloom well in average soil if you water during dry spells. Buy plants at a nursery in spring, sow the seeds outdoors while the soil is still cool, or start seeds indoors 8 weeks before the last frost. Many hollyhocks flower only in their second year, but some bloom the first year and some continue as perennials. They may self-sow or not, depending on variety and growing conditions. Hollyhocks are prone to rust and other fungal diseases and may be attacked by slugs, snails, Japanese beetles, and spider mites.

Dyeing with hollyhocks

Pick the flowers every two or three days. You may store them in a plastic bag in the refrigerator for a week or so, until you have enough to use. Dark rose, red, or black hollyhocks give the most interesting dyes; remove the green calyces and use just the petals.

Don't bother separating the calyces from light pink or yellow hollyhocks as it doesn't affect the results. Cover the flowers with water, simmer for 30 minutes, and strain. The dyebath will be slightly mucilaginous.

To dye, add mordanted yarn, simmer one hour, cool, and rinse. Light-colored hollyhocks give yellows, golds, and browns, varying with mordant. The darker-colored hollyhocks give shades of lilac, purple, mauve, gray-green, and brown, depending on dyebath concentration, pH, fiber, mordant, and how long you simmer and soak the yarn. Try different mordants, dipping dyed skeins in vinegar or ammonia afterbaths to shift the color, or letting the yarn soak in the dyebath for 2 or 3 days at room temperature. Like hardy hibiscus, dark-colored hollyhocks make rich, intriguing, but unpredictable dyebaths.

PALE PASTEL FLOWERS

Alum on wool

Copper on wool

Alum on cotton

DARK ROSE-PINK FLOWERS

Alum on silk

Alum on wool

Alum on wool, ammonia dip

Tin on wool

Purple basil
(*Ocimum basilicum* cultivars)

Tender perennial, grown as an annual. All zones.
Height: 2 feet.
Spacing: 1 plant per square foot.
Yield: The tops of 18 plants can dye 4 ounces of wool.

Description

Seed and herb catalogs list several strains of basil with dark solid purple or splotchy purple-and-green foliage. Some of the most common are 'Dark Opal', 'Purpurascens', 'Purple Ruffles', and 'Red Rubin'. They differ in leaf size, shape, and color, but they're interchangeable for dyeing. All are attractive, upright, bushy plants that branch repeatedly, especially if pruned. The opposite leaves are oval or scalloped, 1 to 3 inches long, with a spicy aroma. Spikes of small but pretty pale pink or lilac flowers cover the top of the plant in late summer and fall.

Related species

Perilla, or shisho (*Perilla frutescens*), is a similar herb, used in Oriental cuisine, that has larger leaves with deep veins and toothed edges. At least one strain has dark purple foliage. Perilla acts the same as purple basil in the dyepot. It's easy to grow and self-sows reliably. Purple perilla is available as plants or seeds from most herb nurseries.

How to grow

Full sun. Purple basil grows best in rich, fertile, moist soil but adapts to average garden soil if you add some compost or fertilizer at planting time and water during dry spells. Choose a site away from taller plants; the purple color doesn't develop well if the leaves are shaded. Start seeds indoors 8 weeks before the last frost and transplant to the garden only after the soil is good and warm, or wait until then and sow directly where the plants are to grow. When the seedlings are a few inches tall, pinch out the tops to promote branching. Cull out any plain green plants.

Dyeing with purple basil

Shear off the tops of the plants anytime during summer or fall and use the material promptly. You can harvest from the same plants every 3 to 5 weeks. Cover with water, simmer for one hour, and strain off the richly aromatic, intensely wine-colored dyebath.

Like those of hibiscus and dark hollyhock flowers, the colors from purple basil are tantalizing but unpredictable. In all three cases, the pigments are anthocyanins, which dissolve easily in water but don't stick readily to yarn. Dyeing with purple basil is especially frustrating because the dyebath makes hard-to-remove stains on stirring rods, floors, sinks, and even stainless steel pans, but it takes prolonged soaking to dye yarn. Simmer mordanted yarn for 1 hour, let it soak for 24 to 48, remove it, and let it dry without rinsing, then wait a few days before washing it. That seems to produce darker colors than washing immediately after dyeing. If you live in a hot climate, purple basil might be a good candidate for solar dyeing: put the yarn and dyebath in a big glass jar and let it simmer in the sun for several days.

Like all anthocyanins, the colors from purple basil shift dramatically in response to pH. Adding vinegar to the dyepot gives purples, mauves, and browns. Adding ammonia to the dyepot (when dyeing cotton) or using an ammonia afterdip (better for silk and wool) gives various shades of green. Using different mordants also affects the results; on wool, I get the darkest, most attractive colors with tin.

WHOLE PLANT TOPS IN FULL BLOOM

Alum on silk

*Alum on cotton,
ammonia dip*

*Alum on wool,
ammonia dip*

*Alum on silk,
pH 7*

*Alum on wool,
vinegar dip*

*Tin on wool,
vinegar dip*

St.-John's-wort
(Hypericum perforatum)

Perennial. Zone 3.
Height: 2 to 3 feet.
Spacing: 1 plant needs 2 square feet.
Yield: The flowers from 24 plants can dye 4 ounces of wool.

Description

St.-John's-wort is an herb native to Europe but widely naturalized in the United States, where it grows along roadsides, on vacant lots, and in abandoned fields and pastures. It makes a clump of many stiff, upright, branching stems lined with pairs of small oval leaves and topped for several weeks in late June and July with clusters of bright yellow flowers. Each flower is about 3/4 inch wide, with a conspicuous tuft of stamens and five petals with black dots along the edges. The fresh flowers steeped in olive oil or alcohol yield a bright red lotion that's a folk remedy for sores, cuts, and minor burns.

Related species

Various species of *Hypericum* may be grown as garden flowers or found as wildflowers or weeds, but St.-John's-wort is the only one to use for dyeing. Too bad the dye pigment isn't produced by any of the species that have larger, easier-to-pick flowers!

How to grow

Full sun. St.-John's-wort is a tough plant that adapts well to dry, infertile, sandy, or gravelly soil. It also thrives in average garden soil, where it gradually spreads to form a patch. It grows readily from seeds, but few suppliers list them. Most herb nurseries sell the plants, though, and you can propagate a single plant by dividing it in spring. Once established, St.-John's-wort needs no care, has no problems, and lives for decades.

Dyeing with St.-John's-wort

Dyeing with St.-John's-wort really isn't practical because you use only the newly opened flowers and you must use them fresh. Picking individual flowers is a slow job, and you need a big patch of plants to get enough flowers for more than a few sample skeins of yarn. Even so, any dyer ought to give St.-John's-wort a try because it behaves so differently from other dyes. I follow the method described by Su Grierson in *The Color Cauldron*.

Pick as many flowers as you can get. This will stain your fingers red but the stain will wash off in a few days. Cover the flowers with water, simmer for an hour, and strain off the deep red dyebath. Add a small skein of alum-mordanted wool, simmer 10 to 15 minutes, remove, and rinse: it will be dyed a medium green. Add a skein of unmordanted wool, simmer one hour, remove, and rinse: it will be a dark mauve-red. Add another alum-mordanted skein and let it soak in the cooling dyebath overnight, remove, and rinse: it will be dark brown or gray. Reheat the dyebath, add another alum-mordanted skein, simmer briefly, remove, and rinse: it will be gold or tan. That's four different colors obtained in sequence from a single dyebath, with just alum or no mordant at all. How remarkable!

On the other hand, whole plant tops, cut in bloom and dried, give only a plain rosy tan. Soaking the flowers (alone) in rubbing alcohol produces a beautiful ruby red solution, but diluting it with water to make a dyebath gives only a drab gold, not the green-red-brown-gold sequence described above. I haven't tried using St.-John's-wort with any mordants other than alum or on any fibers other than wool.

NEWLY OPENED FLOWERS

Alum on wool, 10 minute simmer

Alum on wool, 1-day soak

Alum on wool, alcohol extract

Alum on wool, exhaust

No mordant on wool, 1-hour simmer

Alum on wool, dried tops

Purple loosestrife
(*Lythrum salicaria, L. virgatum,* and hybrids)

Perennial. Zone 3.
Height: up to 5 feet.
Spacing: 1 plant needs 2 square feet.
Yield: The tops of 12 plants can dye 4 ounces of wool.

Description

Purple loosestrife (*Lythrum salicaria*) is a showy European wildflower that has spread to become a major weed of wetlands and marshes in the northern United States and adjacent Canada. It spreads by seeds and by underground runners to form dense patches of tall, slender stems clasped by pairs of slightly hairy leaves and topped with long spikes of rosy purple flowers in late summer. *L. virgatum,* also called purple loosestrife, looks almost identical but has leaves that are smoother and more slender, and is (so far) less of a weed problem. Both species contain tannins, which give unusual shades of brown and black. *L. salicaria,* in particular, has several uses in European folk medicine.

Related species

The common name loosestrife also refers to plants in the unrelated genus *Lysimachia,* but none of them are dye plants.

How to grow

Full sun. Both purple loosestrifes prefer rich, moist soil but grow well in average garden soil if watered during dry spells. You can grow either species from seeds, but the named cultivars sold at perennial nurseries are more compact and have prettier flowers. I like 'Morden Pink', which has clear pink flowers and grows only 2 to 3 feet tall. Harvest the plant tops as soon as the flowers start to fade to use for dyeing and to prevent self-seeding. Propagate named cultivars by dividing the plants in early spring. Purple loosestrife cannot be sold in Minnesota, Washington, and California and may come to be banned throughout the Great Lakes and northeastern states, but it is not (yet) a weed problem across the southern United States.

Dyeing with purple loosestrife

Gather whole plant tops, cutting them close to the ground after most of the flowers have faded. Use them fresh or dry the material for later use. Cover with water, soak overnight, then boil for 2 hours or longer. Strain off the medium-tan dyebath.

To dye, add mordanted yarn, simmer for at least one hour, let the yarn soak in the dyebath overnight, and rinse. Using alum, tin, copper, chrome, or no mordant at all gives various shades of brown. To make black, start with alum-mordanted yarn, simmer one hour and remove the yarn. Dissolve 1/2 teaspoon of iron mordant in a jar of hot water, stirring well, and add it to the dyebath. Put the yarn back in, simmer for another hour, and let it soak overnight before rinsing it.

FLOWERING SHOOTS IN FULL BLOOM

Alum on wool

Alum on silk

Copper on wool

Chrome on wool

Tin on wool

Iron on wool

No mordant on wool

Bronze fennel
(*Foeniculum vulgare* 'Purpurascens')

Hardy perennial, can be grown as an annual. Zone 5.
Height: 3 to 6 feet.
Spacing: 1 plant needs 2 square feet.
Yield: The tops of 8 plants can dye 4 ounces of wool.

Description

Bronze fennel is valued mostly for its beautiful foliage, which has a delicate texture
and unusual purple-bronze or coppery red color. Each compound leaf is divided into
hundreds of tiny segments that are as thin and soft as sewing thread. Early in the season, the new shoots are crowded near the ground in a compact fluffy mound. Later on,
the stalks stretch several feet tall, topped with lacy clusters of tiny yellow flowers.
Flowering continues until fall, and the plants die back to the ground after a few hard
frosts. The leaves and flowers are aromatic and edible and can be added to salads,
sauces, egg dishes, or other foods.

Related species

There are other forms of fennel, all in the same species: Florence fennel, which
makes a swollen bulb that's eaten as a vegetable; sweet fennel, raised for its tasty seeds;
and wild fennel, a weedy form that's common in California. I haven't used it myself,
but I've read that wild fennel gives good yellows and golds in the dyepot.

How to grow

Full sun. Bronze fennel thrives in average garden soil. Water it during dry spells.
You can buy small plants from an herb nursery or raise your own from seeds. Sow them
in individual pots indoors 6 to 8 weeks before the last spring frost, and transplant into
the garden after frost, or wait until the soil is warm and sow seeds in the garden where
you want the plants to grow.

Bronze fennel is a carefree plant. The only common pest is a striped caterpillar;
leave it alone, and it will turn into a swallowtail butterfly. Harvest all you want for dyeing and cut the rest down to the ground in late fall. This herb is a short-lived perennial
that usually dies out after two to four years. It may self-sow but isn't weedy. Watch for

volunteers or raise new seedlings to replace the original planting.

Dyeing with bronze fennel

Gather whole shoots any time from spring to fall and use them fresh. Leaves, stems, and flowers all give the same colors. Cover with water, boil for about 1/2 hour, and strain. The anise-scented dyebath will be a medium gold.

To dye, add mordanted yarn, simmer for 30 minutes or longer, then cool and rinse. Bronze fennel gives a nice range of clear colors that vary with different mordants but are unaffected by vinegar or ammonia. On wool, alum gives a clear yellow, tin a medium brown, and iron a dark green-brown.

WHOLE PLANT TOPS PRIOR TO BLOOM

Alum on silk

Alum on wool

Tin on wool

Iron on wool

Marjoram
(Origanum majorana)

Tender perennial, grown as an annual. All zones.
Height: 1 foot.
Spacing: 2 plants per square foot.
Yield: The tops of 24 plants can dye 4 ounces of wool.

Description

Sweet marjoram is a compact, bushy little plant with soft, oval, gray-green leaves that release a pleasing aroma when you stroke them. In summer, its stems are topped with rounded, knotlike clusters of gray bracts that surround inconspicuous white flowers. Marjoram makes a good edging for the front of a bed and can be clipped like a miniature hedge.

Related species

Several other species of *Origanum* are grown as herbs or ornamentals, but not for dyeing. Historically, dyers have obtained a red or purple dye from the rosy red flowers of wild marjoram, a pretty but weak-scented variety of oregano (*O. vulgare* var. *vulgare*), but obtaining that dye requires a complex process of drying and fermenting the flowers; simply boiling the flowers yields only gold or tan.

How to grow

Full sun. Sweet marjoram grows best in rich, well-drained soil amended with ground limestone. Start the seeds indoors 8 weeks before the last frost or buy transplants at a garden center in spring. Pinch the tops of young plants to induce branching. Water during prolonged dry spells. Sweet marjoram rarely self-sows, so plan to start new plants every year. Although it can survive mild winters, older plants aren't as attractive or productive as young ones.

Dyeing with sweet marjoram

Shear the tops of the plants every 4 to 6 weeks in summer and fall, and use them fresh or dry for later use. Cover with water, simmer for one hour, and strain the fragrant dyebath (unfortunately, the aroma doesn't linger on the dyed yarn).

To dye, add mordanted yarn, simmer for one hour, cool, and rinse. The dyebath is an unpromising dull gold, but using different mordants gives a pleasant array of colors, ranging from yellow and gold to orange, brown, and gray.

Alum on wool

Copper on wool

Chrome on wool

LEAFY SHOOTS AND FLOWER HEADS

Tin on wool

Hops
(Humulus lupulus)

Perennial. Zone 3.
Height: up to 25 feet.
Spacing: 1 plant needs 4 square feet.
Yield: The tops of 2 established vines can dye 4 ounces of wool.

Description

Hops is a vigorous perennial vine that will cover an arbor or trellis with a dense tangle of new growth each summer but dies to the ground in winter. Its twining stems and large, lobed leaves have a harsh, scratchy texture. There are separate male and female plants. The females bear fragrant, puffy, conelike seed heads called strobiles that are used to flavor beer, brew into tea, and stuff into pillows (because their fragrance has a sedative effect). Several cultivars have been selected for beermaking. 'Aureus' is an ornamental cultivar with bright gold foliage.

Related species

Japanese hops (*Humulus japonicus*), used for dyeing in Japan, is an annual species with similar foliage, flowers, and properties.

How to Grow

Full sun. Hops is a tough, long-lived plant that needs little care and thrives in average soil. It puts out fleshy underground runners that may fill a bed; give it a place where it can spread or use edging to confine it. Seeds of perennial hops are not commonly available, but you can buy dormant roots to plant in early spring. Provide a strong trellis or support or let the vine scramble over a shed, fence, or hedge. Wear long sleeves and gloves to protect your arms when you pick stems for dyeing or clean up the debris in fall.

A few companies list seeds of the annual Japanese hops. Usually they offer the variegated form, which has bright white blotches on its leaves. Start the seeds indoors 6 weeks before the last frost or sow directly in the garden when the soil is warm. Plants can grow 10 to 15 feet tall but need a long growing season to reach maturity.

Dyeing with hops

Gather leafy shoots in summer or fall, with or without the flower clusters—any batch of fresh material gives about the same range of colors. Stuff the shoots into a dyepot, cover with water, and simmer for one hour. Hops smells like asparagus or beans as it boils. The shoots will still be tough and stiff when you strain them out, and the dyebath won't appear to have much color.

To dye, add mordanted yarn, simmer for one hour, cool, and rinse. A dyebath made from fresh shoots gives various shades of tan, yellow, gold, olive, khaki, and brown, depending on mordant, fiber, and dyebath concentration. I haven't tried it, but dyeing with dried strobiles might give different results.

MALE AND FEMALE FLOWERS COMBINED

Alum on wool

Alum on silk

Alum on wool, copper dip

Tin on wool

LEAFY SHOOTS PRIOR TO BLOOM

Alum on wool

Alum on silk

Copper on wool

Tin on wool

Peppergrass
(Lepidium ruderale)

Annual. All zones.
Height: 1 to 2 feet.
Spacing: 4 plants per square foot.
Yield: The tops of 24 to 32 plants can dye 4 ounces of wool.

Description

Mark the spot where you sow this plant; otherwise, you'll mistake the seedlings for weeds and pull them out. They have soft-textured, medium green oblong leaves. Weeks after sowing, the stalks bolt up, bear lots of little yellow 4-petaled flowers, then go to seed. Flower arrangers find that the stalks of dried seedpods make an interesting filler for everlasting bouquets.

Related species

More popular in England than in the United States, garden cress (*Lepidium sativum*) and its cultivars are harvested as sprouts to add a peppery flavor to salads or sandwiches, or grown to maturity for everlasting bouquets. As dye plants, they're interchangeable with peppergrass.

How to grow

Full sun. Peppergrass grows in any average garden soil. Sow seeds directly in the garden in early spring before the last frost and thin to 4 to 6 inches apart. Water during dry spells and prop the top-heavy flower stalks with twiggy sticks if needed to keep them from tipping over.

Dyeing with peppergrass

Cut whole plant tops at ground level when they are in full bloom, chop them enough to fit down into the dyepot, cover with water, and boil one hour. Strain off the dyebath, which will look weak and smell fetid.

To dye, add mordanted yarn, simmer one hour, cool, and rinse. Peppergrass gives very nice light to golden yellows on alum-mordanted cotton, silk, and wool. The colors are pure and clear with no tinge of green.

Alum on cotton

WHOLE PLANTS AFTER PEAK BLOOM

Alum on wool

Alum on wool

Alum on wool

Broom sedge
(Andropogon virginicus)

Perennial. Zone 3.
Height: 2 to 3 feet.
Spacing: 1 plant per square foot.
Yield: The tops of 6 plants can dye 4 ounces of wool.

Description

Broom sedge is an extremely tough native grass that's common throughout the eastern United States, where it thrives on disturbed sites such as roadsides, vacant lots, and overgrazed pastures. It forms erect clumps of slender leaves that are purple-green in summer and turn gold or russet after frost. The tiny flowers are inconspicuous when they open in late summer, but they mature into fluffy white seed heads that sparkle when backlit, an effect that's especially lovely in late fall when the sun sinks low in the sky. The dry stems stand up through rain and snowstorms and look good all winter.

Related species

Little bluestem (*Andropogon scoparius*, now renamed *Schizachyrium scoparium*) is a beautiful grass that grows wild across the United States, especially on the Great Plains. Its foliage is blue-green in summer and turns a rich copper in fall and winter. Although rarely cited as a dye plant, it gives rich yellows and golds similar to broom sedge.

Big bluestem, or turkey foot (*A. gerardii*), is a robust prairie grass that forms clumps up to 8 feet tall. It may be a good dye plant, too.

How to grow

Full sun. Broom sedge thrives in average garden soil but tolerates dry, shallow, gravelly, compacted, or nutrient-poor soil. Easy to grow, it persists for years and requires no care. It doesn't spread by runners and self-seeds infrequently.

Perhaps because it's so common in the wild, broom sedge is almost never listed in seed or plant catalogs. Little bluestem is more popular among gardeners and is available from many suppliers. Both broom sedge and little bluestem grow readily from seed and reach blooming size the first year. Propagate established plants by digging and dividing clumps in early spring.

Dyeing with broom sedge

Gather leafy shoots in summer or early fall to use fresh, or dry the leaves to store for later use. Grass gathered in winter gives duller colors. Cover the grass with water, boil for one hour, and strain.

To dye, add mordanted fiber, simmer, cool, and rinse. Simmering for as little as 10 to 15 minutes gives light clear colors; simmering for an hour or longer gives darker but drabber colors. Both broom sedge and little bluestem give a range of yellows and golds on alum-mordanted wool, silk, or cotton.

WHOLE PLANT TOPS IN LATE SUMMER

Alum on wool

Alum on silk

Copper on wool

Tin on wool

Dyer's greenweed, dyer's broom, woadwaxen *(Genista tinctoria)*

Hardy shrub. Zone 4.
Height: less than 2 feet.
Spacing: 1 plant needs 4 square feet.
Yield: The trimmings from 4 plants can dye 4 ounces of wool.

Description

Dyer's greenweed is a low-growing shrub that gradually forms a dense thicket of green twigs. Its slender leaves are inconspicuous, but the small, bright yellow flowers catch your eye in summer. The cultivars 'Flore-Pleno' and 'Royal Gold' have more and larger flowers than average seedlings.

Related species

Genista pilosa 'Vancouver Gold' is similar to but more showy than dyer's greenweed, with generous masses of golden flowers in late spring. Several other species of *Genista* and of the closely related genera *Cytisus* and *Spartium* are also popular garden shrubs; most of them give yellow and gold dyes.

How to grow

Full sun. Dyer's greenweed adapts to good garden soil, but doesn't require it. It's a useful ground cover for hot, dry sites with infertile sandy soil. If you want only one plant, it's easiest to buy a named cultivar from a nursery and set it where you want it. Dyer's greenweed can't be divided and transplants poorly. If you want several plants, you can save money by growing them from seeds. Order a packet of seeds, soak them in warm water overnight, and sow them in individual pots. Wait until the seedlings are a few inches tall before moving them to their permanent locations. They will flower beginning the second year but won't fill in for a few more years.

Dyeing with dyer's greenweed

Cut fresh shoots anytime during the growing season or shear the plant once after flowering and dry the trimmings. Shearing makes the plants more bushy. Don't bother separating stems, leaves, and flowers; they all give the same colors. Cover with water, simmer for one hour, soak overnight, and strain off the dark gold dyebath.

To dye, add mordanted yarn and simmer for 15 minutes or longer. Brief simmering gives clear light yellows on alum-mordanted wool, silk, and cotton. Prolonged simmering gives darker golds. Copper mordant on wool gives a dull green. An iron afterdip on an alum-mordanted skein changes the yellow to a medium brown. Dyer's greenweed contains luteolin, the same yellow pigment that is in weld (page 102), so it gives similar colors. Dyer's greenweed plants live longer than weld, but they grow more slowly and yield less color per square foot of garden space.

LEAFY SHOOTS CUT AFTER FLOWERING

Alum on cotton

Alum on wool

Copper on wool

Tin on wool

Weld
(Reseda luteola)

Biennial or annual. Zone 3.
Height: Flower stalks reach 2 to 4 feet.
Spacing: 2 plants per square foot.
Yield: The rosettes of 12 plants or flowering tops of 6 plants can dye 4 ounces of wool.

Description

Weld is a European dye plant used since Roman times to make a clear yellow that's especially lightfast. Normally a biennial, weld makes a very flat rosette 6 to 10 inches wide of shiny, bright green oblong leaves with wavy or rippled edges. In its first year, the rosette stays green late into the fall or all winter in mild climates. In late spring or early summer of the second year, the plant sends up one or more 2- to 4-foot tall stalks crowded with smaller leaves and little yellowish flowers. Flowering continues for several weeks before the plant goes to seed and dies. If you sow seeds in early spring and the young seedlings are exposed to near-freezing temperatures, however, weld will flower the first year, like an annual.

Related species

Mignonette (*Reseda odorata*) is a cool-season annual that makes a floppy mound of leaves and small tufts of greenish or brownish flowers that have an incredibly sweet and pleasant fragrance. It's not a dye plant.

How to grow

Full sun. Weld thrives in any well-drained garden soil. Water it deeply once a week during hot, dry spells. You can sow seeds indoors or buy started plants from herb nurseries, but these may not transplant well because weld makes a deep taproot. You're likely to get better plants by sowing seeds directly in the garden in spring or early summer. Thin the seedlings to 6 to 8 inches apart. I start new weld plants each spring, use leaves all summer, and discard leftover rosettes in the fall. If you let them mature and bloom, harvest the plants soon after flowering to prevent rampant self-seeding. It's easier to sow the few plants you want than to weed out hundreds you don't want.

Dyeing with weld

Pluck leaves from around the base of first-year rosettes or cut whole flower stalks when they form. Use fresh or dry for later use. Cover with water, simmer one hour, and strain off the gold dyebath. The smell of simmering weld reminds me of asparagus, snap beans, or other green vegetables.

To dye, add mordanted wool, silk, or cotton yarn, simmer 15 to 60 minutes, cool, and rinse. Weld gives a variety of pale and dark yellows, greenish yellows, and golds, varying with mordant, dyebath concentration, and simmering time. Old dye books always recommend using the flower stalks, but I think that using just the rosettes give clearer, prettier colors.

WHOLE PLANTS IN BLOOM

Alum on cotton

Alum on silk

Alum on wool

Alum on wool

Tin on wool

Copper on wool

Chrome on wool

Indigo
(Indigofera suffruticosa)

Tender shrub, grown as an annual. Needs a long, hot summer.
Height: 3 to 6 feet.
Spacing: 1 plant per square foot.
Yield: The leaves of 2 to 4 plants can dye 4 ounces of wool.

Description

This species of indigo is native to Mexico and the Caribbean islands, where it becomes a small shrub with woody stems, but it comes quickly from seed and can be grown as an annual wherever summers are long and hot. It makes a bushy, erect plant, covered with bright green pinnately compound leaves that feel slightly silky. Short spikes of tiny flesh-colored pea-blossom flowers form in the leaf axils in late summer followed by clusters of short, sickle-shaped woody pods.

Related species

The genus *Indigofera* comprises hundreds of species, but the only other one that's significant as a dye plant is *I. tinctoria*, a native of southeast Asia that looks like *I. suffruticosa* but has straight pods. I've grown *I. tinctoria* a few times, but it's never flowered before the first fall frosts, and I've never gotten good dyes from it. I think it needs a longer, hotter growing season than *I. suffruticosa* does.

Don't be deceived by the beautiful blue flowers of *Baptisia australis*, a showy wildflower that's very popular in perennial gardens, nor by the Latin name of *B. tinctoria* ("tinctoria" means "used by dyers", a misnomer in this case), a species with bright yellow flowers that's less common in gardens. Both are called wild indigo or false indigo, but I've never gotten appreciable color from any part of them, and I've never met anyone else who did, either. Grow them for their beauty, not for dyeing.

How to grow

Full sun. Indigo adapts to different soils but does best in fertile, well-drained soil with regular watering. Its most important requirement is hot weather, humid or dry. Wherever cotton, okra, and watermelons thrive, indigo grows well, too. The seeds are listed in a few mail-order catalogs. You may see plants listed, too, but it's better to buy seeds as the plants usually don't travel well. Sow seeds after an overnight soak in warm water, either directly in the garden after the soil is good and warm or indoors in individual pots about 8 weeks before the last frost. Don't put the plants outdoors too soon; if stunted by cold, they don't recover. Other than that, indigo is easy to grow and trouble-free.

Dyeing with indigo

The blue pigment comes only from the leaves—there's none in the stems, roots, or flowers. It reaches maximum concentration when the plants are in bloom. Pick entire leaves from blooming plants anytime in late summer or fall, starting at the base of the plant. You may remove up to one-third of the leaves at a single picking and harvest again at 2-week intervals. Use the fresh leaves immediately, following the directions on pages 42–44.

LEAVES IN MIDSUMMER

silk, 15-minute soak

wool, 15-minute soak

cotton, 30-minute soak

silk, 30-minute soak

wool, 30-minute soak

wool, exhaust

Japanese indigo, dyer's knotweed
(Polygonum tinctorium)

Annual. All zones.
Height: 2 to 3 feet.
Spacing: 1 plant needs at least 2 square feet.
Yield: The leaves of 2 to 4 plants can dye 4 ounces of wool.

Description

Japanese indigo has been used for centuries in Japan and Southeast Asia and gives a blue dye that's identical to the dye from *Indigofera* indigos. It was introduced to the United States by Dorothy Miller, who wrote about it in her book, *Indigo from Seed to Dye*. It branches readily into a full, bushy plant. Like other knotweeds, it has smooth stems with swollen joints and simple alternate leaves. The leaves are normally bright green, but if bruised or frosted, they turn navy blue, revealing the pigment inside. In late summer and fall, slender clusters of tiny bright pink flowers appear.

Related species

There are hundreds of species in the genus *Polygonum*. Some give good yellow or tan dyes. *P. tinctorium* is the only one to use for a blue dye. You'll have to order seeds; this plant doesn't grow wild in North America; in fact, it's quite scarce even in gardens. Don't be deceived by the weedy lookalikes—especially *P. pensylvanicum* and *P. persicaria*—that grow along roadsides and in barnyards and gardens. They don't have what you want.

How to grow

Full sun is best in most areas; provide afternoon shade where summers are very hot. Japanese indigo tolerates average garden conditions, but it prefers rich, moist soil amended with plenty of compost or manure. The better you treat it, the bigger it will get, and the more color it will give. Start the seeds indoors about 6 weeks before the last frost and transplant seedlings into the garden when the soil is warm. Mulch to keep the soil damp and water regularly during dry spells. This plant is easy to grow, and it never has pests or diseases.

Japanese indigo seeds and plants are hard to get, so save your own seeds from year to year. Gather the seedheads when they turn tan, put them in paper bag to dry for a week or so, then rub them between your fingers to press out the seeds. Seal the seeds in a plastic container or glass jar and store them in a cool, dark place. They lose viability quickly, so save fresh seeds every year.

Japanese indigo flowers late and the seeds don't ripen until October at the earliest. If a frost is likely before then, root a few tip cuttings in late summer and grow them on a sunny windowsill. They'll flower indoors and you can collect some seeds, but the potted plants get too straggly to save all winter.

Dyeing with Japanese indigo

The blue pigment comes only from the leaves. Starting at the base of the stems, harvest leaves anytime from midsummer until frost. You can remove up to one-third of the leaves at a single picking and pick every week or two. Wherever you pick off a leaf, a side shoot will develop, so the more you pick, the more you get. Use the fresh leaves immediately, following the directions on pages 42–44.

After extracting the indigo for dyeing blue, you can use the same leaves to give shades of gold, khaki, and brown on wool and silk. Cover the leaves with water, boil for one hour, and strain off the amber dyebath. Add mordanted yarn, simmer for one hour, cool, and rinse.

LEAVES IN SUMMER AS VAT DYE

cotton, 30-minute soak

silk, 30-minute soak

wool, 30-minute soak

wool, 30-minute soak

silk, 15-minute soak

wool, 15-minute soak

wool, exhaust

LEAVES BOILED AFTER EXTRACTING THE INDIGO

Alum on silk

Alum on wool

Copper on wool

Woad
(Isatis tinctoria)

Biennial. Zone 3.
Height: flower stalks reach 2 to 3 feet.
Spacing: 1 plant per square foot.
Yield: The leaves of 24 plants can dye 4 ounces of wool.

Description

Used for many centuries in Great Britain and northern Europe, woad is *the* source of blue for dyers in cold climates. Starting from seed, it makes a low rosette of glossy dark green foliage the first season. The leaves are oblong, 6 to 10 inches long, with smooth or wavy edges. Where winters are mild, woad is evergreen; otherwise, it freezes down to the ground. In the spring, woad flowers as early as daffodils, in the same vivid shade of yellow. Massed at the top of a few sturdy stalks, the thousands of tiny flowers soon form flat, dangling seedpods that darken from light green to almost black as they mature. Woad usually dies after flowering once, but sometimes a few new shoots come up around the base of the plant to keep it going for another year.

Woad looks spectacular in bloom, and the first-year rosettes make a nice low edging for a bed of dye plants. However, it is indicted as a "noxious weed" in some western states where it has invaded rangelands. I think that woad may be a scapegoat, not a culprit; in the sites where I've seen it spread, the native vegetation had already been damaged by overgrazing or development. Whatever the case, gardeners west of the Rockies should check with a local extension agent before planting woad.

Related species

The genus contains about thirty species, but this is the only one commonly grown in gardens and the only one acknowledged as a dye plant.

How to grow

Full sun. In its weedy way, woad adapts to almost any soil and site, but for best results, plant it in rich, deep soil amended with plenty of compost or manure. Use mulch to keep the soil cool and moist, and water regularly. Treated this way, woad makes mounded rosettes up to 18 inches wide. The more leaves, the more dye. Many herb catalogs offer woad seeds. You can start seedlings indoors and transplant them, but it works just as well to sow seeds outdoors as soon as the ground can be worked. Sow them 1/2 inch deep, and thin the seedlings to stand 12 to 18 inches apart. After harvesting leaves all summer, I usually dig and discard the plants in fall. Let them overwinter if you want to see them bloom, but then cut them back immediately. Leave one stalk if you want to save some fresh seeds (stored seeds remain viable for a few years), but don't let all the seeds ripen and scatter at random or you'll have woad woes.

Dyeing with woad

For dyeing, pick leaves from the first-year rosettes anytime from midsummer until early fall. Use them immediately, following the directions on pages 42–44. Woad leaves don't give much blue after frost in fall, and they're useless in the second year. Woad produces the same blue pigment as indigo or Japanese indigo, but is less concentrated (you'll need four times as much woad) and produces dustier blues.

Woad does give a second color that is interesting and unusual. After extracting the blue, you can use the same leaves to get shades of pink or pinkish beige. Cover them with water, simmer for an hour, and strain off the dyebath. Add mordanted wool, simmer for an hour, and rinse.

LATE-SUMMER LEAVES AS VAT DYE

wool, 20–minute soak

wool, 30–minute soak

wool, 45–minute soak

Wool, 10–minute soak

LATE-SUMMER LEAVES BOILED

Alum on wool

Copper on wool

SUPPLIERS

Mail-order suppliers of dye plants and seeds

Although no single nursery supplies all the dye plants described in this book, the following each offer one or more kinds, either as seeds or as baby plants. Visiting the websites is the quickest and easiest way to determine what plants are available and place an order. Some nurseries don't have websites; in those cases, I've included the price for ordering a printed catalog.

Abundant Life Seeds
PO Box 157
Saginaw, OR 97472
www.abundantlifeseed.org

Blessing Historical
  Foundation
Box 517
Blessing, TX 77419
Send $5 for a packet of
  madder seeds

Chiltern Seeds
Bortree Stile
Ulverston, Cumbria,
  England LA12 7PB
www.chilternseeds.co.uk

Companion Plants
7247 N. Coolville Ridge Rd.
Athens, OH 45701
www.companionplants.com

Flowery Branch Seed
  Company
PO Box 1330
Flowery Branch, GA 30542
Catalog $4

The Fragrant Path
PO Box 328
Ft. Calhoun, NE 68023
Catalog $2

Goodwin Creek Gardens
PO Box 83
Williams, OR 97544
www.goodwincreekgardens.
  com

Greenfield Herb Garden
PO Box 9
Shipshewana, IN 46565
www.the-herb-garden.com

Herbfarm
14590 NE 145th St.
Woodinville, WA 98072
www.herbfarm.com

Johnny's Selected Seeds
955 Benton Ave.
Winslow, ME 04901
www.johnnyseeds.com

J. L. Hudson, Seedsman
Star Route 2, Box 337
La Honda, CA 94020
www.jlhudsonseeds.net

Native Seeds/SEARCH
526 N. 4th Ave.
Tucson, AZ 85705
www.nativeseeds.org

Park Seed Company, Inc.
1 Parkton Ave.
Greenwood, SC 29647
www.parkseed.com

Plants of the Southwest
3095 Agua Fria Rd.
Santa Fe, NM 87507
www.plantsofthesouthwest.
  com

Richters Herb Specialists
357 Highway 47
Goodwood, Ontario
Canada L0C 1A0
www.richters.com

Sandy Mush Herb Nursery
316 Surrett Cove Rd.
Leicester, NC 28748
www.sandymushherbs.com

Stokes Seed Company
PO Box 548
Buffalo, NY 14240
www.stokeseeds.com

Thompson & Morgan
PO Box 1308
Jackson, NJ 08527
www.thompson-morgan.com

Well-Sweep Herb Farm
317 Mt. Bethel Rd.
Port Murray, NJ 07865
www.wellsweep.com

Mail-order suppliers of mordants and dried dye plants

Carolina Homespun
455 Lisbon St.

San Francisco, CA 94112
www.carolinahomespun.com

Dharma Trading Company
PO Box 150916
San Rafael, CA 94915
www.dharmatrading.com

Earth Guild
33 Haywood St.
Asheville, NC 28801
www.earthguild.com

Earthsong Fibers
5115 Excelsior Blvd., #428

Minneapolis, MN 55416
www.earthsongfibers.com

The Mannings
PO Box 687
East Berlin, PA 17316
www.the-mannings.com

The Woolery
PO Box 468
Murfreesboro, NC 27855
www.woolery.com

BIBLIOGRAPHY

Adrosko, Rita J. *Natural Dyes and Home Dyeing.* New York: Dover 1971.

Bliss, Anne. *North American Dye Plants.* Loveland, Colorado: Interweave Press, 1993.

Brunello, Franco, translated by Bernard Hickey. *The Art of Dyeing in the History of Mankind.* Cleveland, Ohio: Phoenix Dyeworks, 1978.

Buchanan, Rita. *A Weaver's Garden.* Loveland, Colorado: Interweave Press, 1987.

Buchanan, Rita, ed. *Dyes from Nature.* Brooklyn, New York: Brooklyn Botanic Garden, 1990.

Cannon, John, and Margaret Cannon. *Dye Plants and Dyeing.* Portland, Oregon: Timber Press, 1994.

Grae, Ida. *Dyes from Nature.* New York: Macmillan, 1974.

Grierson, Su. *The Colour Cauldron.* Loveland, Colorado: Interweave Press, 1986.

Liles, James. *The Art and Craft of Natural Dyeing.* Knoxville, Tennessee: University of Tennessee Press, 1990.

McRae, Bobbi A. *Colors from Nature.* Pownal, Vermont: Storey Communications, 1993.

____. *Nature's Dyepot.* Austin, Texas: Fiberworks Publications, 1991.

Miller, Dorothy. *Indigo from Seed to Dye.* Aptos, California: Indigo Press, 1984.

Schetky, Ethel Jane, ed. *Dye Plants and Dyeing.* Brooklyn, New York: Brooklyn Botanic Garden, 1964.

Weigle, Palmy, ed. *Natural Plant Dyeing.* Brooklyn, New York: Brooklyn Botanic Garden, 1973.

Van Stralen, Trudy. *Indigo Madder & Marigold.* Loveland, Colorado: Interweave Press, 1993.

INDEX

additives and afterdips 41

black-eyed susan 70–71
bronze fennel 90–91
broom sedge 98–99

color variation 45–47
coreopsis 58–59

dahlia 60–61
daisy-shaped garden 22–23
dyebath additives and
    afterdips 41
dyebath, making 39 -40
dyeing, equipment and
    facilities 33
dyeing yarn 40–41
dyer's broom 100–101
dyer's chamomile 72–73
dyer's coreopsis 56–57
dyer's greenweed 100–101
dyer's knotweed 106–107

equipment and facilities for
    dyeing 33
exhaust bath 41

garden basics 20
garden, daisy-shaped 22–23
    mixed-border 26–27
    planning on paper 21–22
    production 28–29
    raised-bed 24–25
garland chrysanthemum
    64–65
gathering plants 38–39
golden marguerite 72–73
goldenrod 66–67

hardy hibiscus 80–81
harvest, first year from seed
    15
hollyhock 82–83
hops 94–95

indigo 104–105
    dyeing with 42–44
invasive plants, controlling 19

Japanese indigo, 106–107
    dyeing with 42–44

madder 52–53
marigold 62–63
marjoram 92–93
mixed-border garden 26–27
mordant, for cellulose fibers
    36–37
mordant, measuring 37
mordant, most common 35
mordant, for protein fibers 36
mordant, reusing and
    disposing 38
mordanting 34–37

peppergrass 96–97
perennials, propagating by
    division 17–19
plants, gathering and storing
    38–39
plants not to grow 11–12
production garden 28–29
propagating, perennials by
    division 17–19
purple loosestrife 88–89
purple basil 84–85

questions and answers 6–8

raised-bed garden 24–25
rose mallow 80–81

seeds, growing plants from
    14–17
    ordering by mail 13–14
    raising seedlings indoors
    14–16
    saving 17
    sowing in the garden 16
spacing of plants 30–31
St.-John's-wort 86–87
storing plants 38–39
sunflower 74–75

tansy 68–69
top-dyeing 47

weedy plants, controlling 19
weld 102–103
woad, 108–109
    dyeing with 42–44
woadwaxen 100–101

yarn, choosing and preparing
    33–37
    dyeing 40–41
yarrow 76–77
yellow cosmos 54–55
yellow bedstraw 50–51
yield of plants 10–11, 30–31

zinnia 78–79